15
k

THE CULINARY RECIPES OF MEDIEVAL ENGLAND

THE CULINARY RECIPES OF MEDIEVAL ENGLAND

An epitome of recipes from extant
medieval English culinary manuscripts

COMPILED AND TRANSLATED

by

Constance B. Hieatt

PB

PROSPECT BOOKS

2013

First published in 2013 by Prospect Books,
Allaleigh House, Blackawton, Totnes, Devon TQ9 7DL.

© 2013, the estate of Constance B. Hieatt.

The author, Constance B. Hieatt, asserts her right to be identified as editor of this work in accordance with the Copyright, Designs & Patents Act 1988.

BRITISH LIBRARY CATALOGUING IN PUBLICATION DATA:
A catalogue entry of this book is available from the British Library.

Typeset by Tom Jaine.

ISBN 978-1-909248-30-4

Printed and bound by the Gutenberg Press, Malta.

Table of Contents

Publisher's Note   7

Introduction   9

CHAPTER ONE

Basic Preparations and Procedures   15

CHAPTER TWO

Meatless Pottages   23
    Based on almond milk   23
    Based on nuts and flowers   28
    Based on eggs   30
    Other meatless pottages   31

CHAPTER THREE

Pottages Based on Grains, Vegetables, or Fruit   33
    Grains   33
    Vegetables   34
    Fruit   41

CHAPTER FOUR

Meat- and Fish-based Pottages   47
    Meat-based   47
    Fish-based   64

CHAPTER FIVE

Special Types of Pottages   71
    Brewets   71
    Sliced dishes   78
    Gruels and sops   85
    Jellied dishes   89
    Pasta   90

CHAPTER SIX

Meat and Game Cooked and Served other than in Pottage   93

CHAPTER SEVEN

Poultry and Feathered Game Cooked and Served
other than in Pottage   109

CHAPTER EIGHT

Fish Cooked and Served other than in Pottage   121

CHAPTER NINE

Eggs and Dairy Dishes   139

CHAPTER TEN

Sauces and Condiments   147

CHAPTER ELEVEN

Baked Dishes   157

CHAPTER TWELVE

Fritters and other Fried Specialities   173

CHAPTER THIRTEEN

Subtleties and Drinks   183

CHAPTER FOURTEEN

Wafers and Confections   189

Bibliography   197

Index of Recipes   203

Publisher's Note

It is a matter of much sadness to record Constance Hieatt's death in December 2011. She worked on this book during her last illness but its organization and presentation for publication were tasks undertaken by her sister, Ellen Nodelman. I am extremely grateful to Ms Nodelman for all the work she has willingly shouldered. I am also grateful to Professor Brenda Hosington for her supervisory eye on the text as it was prepared for the press.

Tom Jaine

Introduction

When Tom Jaine first suggested to me that I compile a book of all medieval English culinary recipes, I thought this was an impossible idea, given the enormous number of them documented in my *Concordance of English Recipes: Thirteenth Through Fifteenth Centuries* (with Terry Nutter and Johnna H. Holloway, published by the Arizona Center for Medieval and Renaissance Studies, 2006). However, when I thought about this later on, I realized it was not so impossible after all: the great majority of these recipes exist in two or more, sometimes a great many more, versions. To make sense of what might be an almighty muddle, in my *Concordance* (and in the later instalment included in my *Cocatrice and Lampray Hay*) these recipes were ordered according to standardized lemmas. Thus there are ten different recipes for caudle of almonds, each with a slightly different, or differently spelled, name, but all under the one lemma of Caudle of Almonds. What I have done, then, is to choose the most basic version of every recipe; if there are truly significant variants, such as a fish version for 'fasting' days, they are generally given in a footnote.

Choosing 'the most basic version' often meant choosing an early one, since many elaborations crept into later versions of popular recipes. In some cases, however, it was simply a matter of choosing the most correct. For example, in a recipe for which there were two exemplars, one called for toasting the bread before soaking it in vinegar, whereas the second reversed this order – which clearly wouldn't do: you can't toast bread which is soaking wet. Of course, when there is an error in a recipe which has no second exemplar, I could only point out the error.

In a few cases, my choice was the version which was most explicit about quantities; medieval recipes are usually vague in this regard, so those which are at all explicit, even partially, are very helpful. An example is the recipe chosen to represent that favourite dish 'Blancmanger': unlike the other

9

twenty-odd recipes for this dish, it tells us to use one part almonds to two parts of rice. That doesn't solve all problems in recreating the dish, but it certainly gives a good starting point.

How to list the recipes was a further problem; simply listing them in alphabetical order would have been of little help to readers looking for particular kinds of recipes. The English culinary collections which divide their recipes into perceptible sections make a useful distinction in indicating the methods of cooking: the one best known to the general public, BL MS Harley 279,[1] has three captioned divisions: 'Potages Dyvers', 'Leche Vyaundez', and 'Vyaunde Furnez'.

Not that these captions explain all. 'Pottages', as used in these culinary texts – and in many menus, both historical and 'suggested' – means primarily soups and stews: foods cooked in a pot and served in a liquid or sauce composed, at least in part, of the liquid in which they were cooked. Sometimes the menus refer to gelled dishes as pottages, so apparently the change effected by cooling (and thus gelling) the liquid did not change the category. On the other hand, other foods cooked in a pot but further treated so that they could be served in slices were generally listed under the category of 'Sliced Foods' although they seem to have started off as pottages. The category of 'Baked Foods' included all kinds of pastries, from fish or roasts of meat baked in a pastry crust down to dainty tarts; but no dishes without pastry are included, so it does not include bread or everything else we would consider 'baked foods' today.

Notice that some large categories of food do not appear here at all: we must thus consider the groupings suggested in various other manuscripts. Bodleian MS Rawlinson D 1222 is incomplete, so that not all of its sections are marked, but those that are seem to be in a logical 'menu' order: 'Sawce', 'Divers fysshes boyled', 'Bakemetes', 'Lechemetes', and 'Ffryed metes'.[2] Cambridge University Library LL.I.18 inserts, after the first 134 miscellaneous recipes, the heading, 'Here bygynneth the rolle and the Ordinance off sleyng of al maner wyldfole, off hole fete and clofe

---

1.   For bibliographical details on the manuscripts mentioned, see the Bibliography.
2.   'Logical menu order' in that sauces, considered to be the essential element in any well-planned meal, come first, while 'fryed foods', primarily fritters, were always among the last on a menu. All the others would have appeared earlier, in something like the mentioned order.

fete, and sawsing for hem, and the sleyng off fowr foted bestes and the sawsing for hem, &ct'. Twenty-three such recipes follow; then we get a new rubric, 'Here begynneth the rosteynge off fysshe and the sethynge and the sawcynge off hem as yt is here after wryten', and 18 recipes for fish. The list ends, without any further caption, with five more recipes, only one of which deals with fish.

Other English collections often give similar descriptions of the sections into which they are divided – but not always: the Forme of Cury has no such headings, but it does group a few fritters, and, somewhat later, a group of recipes for 'subtleties' of one sort or another, both in the correct 'menu' order. It thus seemed reasonable to divide this collection of all kinds of English recipes into groupings that follow both menu order and distinctions in type of cooking. Thus the overall divisions are Preliminaries; Pottages; Main Courses; and Special Dishes.

Preliminaries (Chapter 1) include mostly directions for making basic ingredients, such as almond milk, rather than the dishes for the table in which these will be used. It also includes general, overall directions, such as instructions to boil onions before using them in most dishes.

The second category, pottages (Chapters 2–6), is much the largest, as it is by far the largest of Harley 279's three categories (104 recipes, as against 64 for 'Sliced Foods' and 61 for 'Baked Foods'). This does not actually mean that people of the social levels represented by our recipes ate more pottages than, say, roasts: the recorded menus and household records suggest rather the opposite. However, almost every course of a menu, no matter how grand, began with a pottage, or, sometimes, two or even three; and the few that did not start that way included at least one later on.

Here we have the origin of our serving soup as a first course for a formal meal: not all 'pottages' were liquid enough to qualify as 'soups' by our standards, but they were all considered to be in the same category then. Clearly, the modern French word for soup, *potage*, attests to the simplification of the category in France, too; pottages also were prominent on French menus, although the order there was not always exactly the same. But why was a 'pottage' so desirable in England as the start of a meal? Perhaps at least one reason was that they were valued for their almost endless variety, in contrast to the relative similarity of most roast and broiled meats and fish.

The variety of pottages which the corpus of Middle English recipes contained turned out to be so very large that it was necessary to divide the pottages here into three main subdivisions and a number of sub-categories, such as 'Vegetables' and 'Gruels and Sops', 'sops' being the dishes (broth with bread to sop it up, basically) which eventually gave us the standard English word for 'soup'. Some may be surprised to find 'fruit' as a category of pottage, but many fruits were boiled and served in their own syrup, and some menus list such fruits as 'pears in syrup' at the beginning of a course where a pottage would be expected.

The third broad category of 'Main Dishes' (Chapters 6–9) contains more dishes, generally meats, fish, or eggs, than there are pottages. Within each chapter, the order is usually approximately alphabetical, often by main ingredient, such as beef. This division into sub-categories, of one sort or another, also seemed to help clarify other sections of the text – but given the size of the base, many difficulties remained. Many recipes were hard to place. Meats and fish in sauces, for example, may or may not be pottages. In general, however, Chapters 6, 7 and 8 will be found to contain largely roasts and grilled or fried dishes served with separately prepared sauces.

Recipes which the title says are for 'brawn' were among the most tricky here, since they had to be distributed among three different categories. 'Brawn' later came to mean primarily a dish of ground boar's meat or pork cooked as a sort of meatloaf and meant to be served sliced; all such dishes are listed as 'Sliced Dishes' in Chapter 5. But 'brawn' also often meant simply the meat from which the sliced dish was made, and some of these dishes are clearly pottages. One recipe, however, is for sliced cooked boar (or pork) in a sauce: which is not a pottage and couldn't really be counted as a 'Sliced Dish' in the usual sense; it will thus be found listed under 'Meats'.

'Special Dishes' (Chapters 10–14), start with sauces: sauces are 'special' because medieval cooks, and diners, thought their main courses, and some other foods, were not fit to eat without a suitable sauce – although some recipes specify, for certain meats, 'No sauce but salt'. Thus, sauces ought to come directly after meat and fish main dishes. Aside from those served with nothing but salt, the only foods which were always served without a separately prepared sauce were those in pottages – which had their own sauces, by their very nature.

The other 'special' dishes are mainly ones which come at or near the end of the menu, although 'Baked Dishes' (Chapter 11) may appear in any of the standard three courses. 'Subtleties' (Chapter 13) had their place at the end of a course, especially the last one of a meal. Fritters and the like (Chapter 12) were considered treats, and always came near the very end of a meal, while confections (Chapter 14) and drinks (Chapter 13) could appear at many times of the day, but were not a normal part of the dinner menu: the drinks served at table were ale and wine. Special drinks were often served after the end of a meal, often accompanied by wafers and confections of various kinds.

The recipe which was most difficult to place was the simplest one: salad. By definition, a green salad does not need cooking, and thus does not fit into any of the 'cooking' categories; I finally decided to put it in the category of 'Sauces and Condiments' (Chapter 10), on the grounds that some condiments may not require cooking either, and all that requires much attention from a cook for a salad is the dressing (a 'sauce'). Other placements which may seem odd include aquavite, a sort of brandy, which is not listed under drinks because it was rarely regarded as a drink in itself in this period. It was, rather, an ingredient added to less potent drinks, such as braggot, to give them more heft, and it was used for flaming effects at the table – as brandy often is today. It is therefore listed among the basic preparations of Chapter 1.

Those who have looked at the *Concordance* and who think I have omitted a few recipes are advised that some of the recipes listed there under separate lemmas are actually elaborated versions of other dishes; for example, 'Hot Almond Milk' is simply almond milk heated up, and 'Apples Royal' is a version of 'Applemoys' with a number of added touches also found in several of the recipes listed under 'Applemoys'. The recipes mentioned by title in footnotes to other recipes, as 'Apples Royal' is, are listed in the index of recipes, but I could not list all recipes referred to in collective references without specific titles.

Some readers may be disappointed that I have not given suggestions for modern adaptations of any of these recipes. There simply is no room for that, given the bulk of a more-or-less 'complete' collection of English recipes. Those who want such help are referred to my earlier books, especially *Pleyn Delit: Medieval Cookery for Modern Cooks* (with Sharon

Butler and Brenda Hosington, 2nd revised edition, University of Toronto Press, 1996) and *An Ordinance of Pottage* (Prospect Books, 1988), both of which contain adaptations of a number of the recipes here collected. Many others here are of dubious appeal to, or practicality for, modern cooks: those who think they want to try one of the versions of 'haggis' would first have to possess themselves of a sheep's stomach to cook it in, for example.

The source of each recipe in this epitome is given at the end of its translation. The abbreviated references are explained in the Bibliography, pages 197–201 below, which identifies the printed or manuscript source of the original text. The notation after the comma in any single reference denotes either the recipe or the page number in the source referred to.

CONSTANCE B. HIEATT
OCTOBER, 2011

CHAPTER ONE

Basic Preparations and Procedures

The 'recipes' in this section are, mostly, for substances to be used later in recipes for food to be served at the table. Many are, thus, for such basic ingredients as a wheat starch and clarified honey, as well as almond milk and rice flour. 'Farsure' for making meatballs is included here as a primary ingredient in many things, beyond the basic 'meatball'. The only spice powder for which a recipe is provided is, unfortunately, neither the 'mild spice powder' nor the 'strong spice powder' frequently called for in recipes, but at least this 'white powder' is called for a few times.

Others are for preserving foods for later use, including directions for drying beans, preserving fruits in honey, and salting venison and a lamprey. Of course, these methods of preserving were far more widely used than just the examples given here, as were some others which may seem more unlikely, such as preserving fresh peapods by burying them in a pot of water. Other 'recipes' here are suggestions for coping with such kitchen problems as burnt or overly salty food. And some are suggestions either simple, such as putting salt in the food, or more complex, like cooking without fire: which seems more a stunt than the solution to a problem.

Almond Butter

Take thick almond milk and boil it, and as it boils add a little wine or vinegar, and then pour it on a piece of canvas and let the whey drain out. Then gather it up with your hands and hang it up for the time it takes to walk a mile, and afterward put it in cold water, and serve it forth. (UC, 7)

Almond Cream

[Recipes start out with exactly the same directions as those for 'Almond Butter', but finish more or less as follows:] Put it in a bowl and dilute it with white wine. Beat it with a saucer until it is as soft as you want it to be. (OP, 103)

Almond Milk

Take broken sugar,[1] or lacking that take clarified honey, and put it into clean water and set it on the fire and boil it, and skim it clean; and set it beside the fire and let it cool. Then blanch your almonds; put them in a mortar and crush them fine. Mix them with this water (P1047, 32)

Amydon (Wheat starch)

Take wheat and steep it nine days, and change the water every day. Pound it well in a mortar until it is quite fine. Dilute it. Boil it in a great deal of water and strain it through a hair sieve, then let it stand and cool. Pour out the water. Lay it on a cloth and turn it over until it is dry.[2] (GK, 3)

Aquavite (Brandy)

Fill your vial full of dregs of strong wine, and add to it these spices all ground: cinnamon, cloves, ginger, nutmeg, galingale, cubebs, grain of paradise,[3] long pepper, black pepper. Also caraway, sermountain, cumin, fennel, smallage, parsley, sage, mint, rue, calamint, oregano: a half ounce or more or less, as you like; pound them a little, for that will be better, and add them to the spice powders. Then put your glass on the fire:[4] set it on the hovel, and make sure the heat does not come out of it; put a vial under it to keep the liquid. (GK, 7)

Beans, Dried

Take white beans. Put them in running water for two days, and change the water. Take them and lay them to dry, then dry them hard on a stone or on a kiln. Then shell them in a mill, and discard the hulls, and cut the beans into two or four pieces at the most; then make them clean. Thus you can keep them as long as you wish. (OP, 2)

1. I.e., broken off a loaf.
2. This starch is not available, or easy to make, today. A medieval cook in need of a substitute would have used rice flour: see directions for making this below.
3. *Amomum Melequetta.*
4. The directions are, of course, for a still.

Burnt Food, Amendment of

Take two or three small bags and fill them full of malt, and sew them firmly closed. Take out the [burned] food and put it in a clean pot, and then hang these bags in the food. Make sure they do not touch the bottom of the pan, and let them boil there a good while, and stir it well, and let it cool. (H5401, 55)

Butter Clarified

Take good fresh water, as much water as you have butter; set the water on the fire in a clean pan and be sure there is no smoke, and when the water is nearly hot put in the butter, and take a good spatula and stir it well until the water begins to boil; then take it and set it away from the fire, and skim it clean, and then let it stand until it is almost cold. Then put it in a basin with a little water, and pour the butter from the hot water, and salt it. You can keep this butter in safekeeping for three or four years, but keep it cold and enclosed. (H5401, 95)

[Cheese]: to Soften Cheese that is too Hard

Lay the cheese wrapped all around with fresh green nettles, and put it to lie still on a good board or on a floor, and within four days it will be soft and fresh. (H5401, 13)

Cherries, Bullace or Plums, Preserving

To keep these fresh until Christmas, take an earthen pot and put honey in it, and take cherries, plums, or bullace, and do not bruise them, and put them in the honey, then cover them with more honey, and cover the pot and set it away from the air; and at Christmas, wash them clean with water and serve them. (TCC 83)

Cooking without Fire

Take a small earthenware pot with an earthenware lid, which must be as wide as the pot; then take another pot of the same earthenware, with a lid like that of the first: this pot is to be deeper than the first by five fingers and wider in circumference by three. Then take pork and chickens' meat and cut into fair-sized pieces, and take fine spices and add them, and salt.

Take the small pot with the meat in it and place it upright in the large pot; cover it with the lid and stop it with moist, clayey earth, so that nothing may escape. Then take unslaked lime and put in the large pot and fill it with water, ensuring that no water enters the small pot; let it stand for the time it takes to walk between five and seven leagues, and then open your pots, and you will find your food indeed cooked. (AN A, 6)

Farsure for Golden Meatballs and other things (Pommedorry)

Take the meat of pork raw and grind it small. Make it up with eggs and strong spice powder, saffron, and salt, and add currants. Make balls of it and wet it well in white of eggs, and put it to boil in boiling water. Take them up and put them on a spit. Roast them well, and take ground parsley and mix it with eggs and some flour, and let it run about the spit. And if you will, take saffron for parsley, and serve it forth.[5] (FC, 182)

Flour to Thicken Sauce

Take dry flour; enclose it in a pastry shell and bake it until it is hard. You can keep this for five years and blend it with many foods. (LCC, 80)

Flour, Rice

Take rice and wash the grains clean; then dry them well in the sun until they are dry. Then grind them small enough and sift them through a linen sieve, or if you do not have a sieve, a strainer. (H279 LV, 22)

Herbs, Preserved

Take flour and build good pastry cases, standing well up; take stalks of sage and fill one full right up to the top, then close the lid fairly and well, so that no bit of air can go out. Do the same with savory, parsley, and rue; and then bake them hard, almost until burnt. Afterward, keep them dry and attend to them. This powder will have more virtue than when it grew on open earth. (LCC, 79)

---

5.   Some recipes for 'Pommedorry' call for beef rather than pork. – The parsley-based finish would have given 'green apples', while the saffron, plus eggs, would give 'golden' ones. Some directions tell us to insert a clove to suggest the stem of the apple.

Honey, Clarified

Take honey and put it in a pot, and add egg white with a little water, and beat it well together with a stick and set it on the fire and boil it; then take it off and let it cool, and when it is almost cold take off the white with a spatula, and serve it forth. (H5401, 93)

Lamprey, (to) Salt

Take a lamprey and stuff it well with salt, and take a good thick canvas and thick lees of wine and lay them on it; then take the lamprey and bury it in the lees, and roll the canvas together and leave it in a place where only a little air enters: and so you shall have it good throughout the year. (Ar 334, 201)

Meat, to Fasten two Pieces

Take a piece of fresh meat and put it in a pot to boil it; or take a piece of fresh meat and carve it all into gobbets: put it in a pot to boil, and take the juice of comfrey and put it in the pot with the meat and it will soon fasten together, and so serve it forth.[6] (FC, 198)

Milk, against Curdling

Add to it a little flour, and stir it well. (H5401, 2)

Onions, Minced

Boil them in clean water before they go into anything except 'alows' [meat 'birds']. (A1393, 27)

Pastry, Short

If you would have the pastry you bake with short and supple, knead it with good ale and it will be short.[7] (SA, 3)

---

6.   Perhaps the first 'piece' should be 'two pieces'?
7.   Presumably 'short' means friable, easily crumbled, not 'rich', as in modern usage.

Peapods, Preserved

Gather peapods a day before time to gather peapods. Boil water and salt together and skim it clean; put it in an earthen pot. Make a hole in the earth and set this pot in it up to the neck. Put these peapods in the pot; lay a stone tile over the pot to press down the peapods. Then take a length of linen cloth. Take water and flour and boil them together, then spread this cloth on a board, put the water and flour on it, and let it become cold. Then spread it above the pot. Find a suitable colour of orpiment[8] and lay [it?] above the canvas. A day and a night before you want to serve them, hang them in a basket in a well and there shake them from the salt. Then take and boil them and serve forth. (CCC, 20)

Pears, Preserved

Take pears and peel them and boil in water over the fire until they are somewhat soft, then take them off and allow to dry; put them in a pot. Then take lightly clarified honey and put it in the pot with the pears until the honey floats on the top; then allow the pot, covered so that the air does not get in, to settle for six days. After six days, pour the honey out of the pot off the pears into a clean pot, and put it over the fire and boil it until the moisture is used up. To test when the honey is cooked enough, put a drop of honey on the thumbnail with a sword, and if it stands and does not spread out it is cooked.

Put that honey back into the pot with the pears and let it stand for ten or twelve days, then take it out and boil it as before, and let it stand as long as before; pour the honey out of the pot again and put it in a pan and add one quart of freshly skimmed honey, six ounces of red sandalwood, four ounces of gum arabic, and one pint of good wine, and boil all these, well combined, for half a quarter of an hour; then add a powder of the spices listed below to be combined with the aforesaid liquid: four ounces of cleaned anise; one ounce each of caraway, dill, and prepared coriander; four ounces each of cinnamon, ginger, grain of paradise, long pepper; two ounces each of mace, cloves, nutmeg, galingale, cardamom, aloeswood; three drams of spikenard.

---

8.   A gold dye.

Let the powder be made and combined with the honey away from the heat of the fire, then put it in the pot with the pears. All fruits can be prepared in this way, and the roots of all plants.[9] (G&C, 2)

Raisins and Currants

All raisins and currants should be picked clean and put in water with a little heat so that they will become round. (A1393, 25)

Rice Flour *see* Flour, Rice

Salt

Cast salt in all things. (A1393, 26)

Salty Food, Amendment of

Take oatmeal and bind it in a fine linen cloth, and let it hang in the pot so that it does not touch the bottom, and let it hang there a good while; and then set it away from the fire and let it cool, and it shall be fresh enough without any manner of liquid added to it.[10] (DS, 49)

Sugar, Clarified

Take a quart of clean water and put it in a pan, and add to it the white of three eggs; and take a brush made of birch boughs and beat the water and the eggs together until they are completely mixed and cast a great scum above. Then put away the birch boughs and add to it two pounds of sugar, and mix all together. Then set it over the fire on a furnace, and when it begins to boil withdraw your fire and do not let it rise; clarify it thus with a low fire. And when it becomes fair and clear in the middle, take it from the fire and strain it through a good strainer, and in the straining hold your brush before the side of the pan to keep the scum from coming down into the strainer. And with that sugar you may make all sorts of confections. (GK, 11)

---

9. Compare the much simpler recipe for preserving cherries or plums in honey, above; this more complex one was probably more reliable for larger fruits and vegetables.
10. The other two recipes for amending this problem are less convincing.

Venison, Preserved

If you want to keep the tail of a deer fresh and in season over the year, or other venison if need be, press out the blood, for that is the cause of much rotting; put it in an earthen pot and cover it with good honey, so that the honey stands over the meat two fingers thick; bind the mouth with leather and keep it from air, sun, or wind in a coffer or hutch or dark cellar. (LCC, 77)

Venison, Salt

Take venison when it is new and cover it hastily with fern so that no wind may come to it, and when you have covered it well take it home and put it in a cellar where neither sun nor wind may come to it, and dismember it, and put it in clean water and leave it there half a day; afterward, put it on hurdles to dry, and when it is dry take salt, and do what your venison requires and put it to boil in water that is as salt as water of the sea, and much more. And after, let the water be cold, so it will be thin, and then put the venison in the water and let it be there three days and three nights; and after, take it out of the water and salt it with dry salt right well in a barrel, and when your barrel is full, cover it hastily so that no sun or wind may come to it. (DS, 57)

Venison, Spoiled, to Restore

To restore spoiled venison, take the spoiled venison and put it in cold water, and afterward make a hole in the hearth and leave it there three days and three nights; after, take it up and rub it well with great saltpetre, there where the spoiling is, and after that let it hang in rain water all night or more. (DS, 58)

White Powder

Take half a pound of loaf sugar and one spoonful of ground ginger; wash your mortar and pestle and heat them well so that they blend the ingredients well together. Test with your mouth whether it is hot enough, and if it is not add more ginger and work it over again, and keep your pestle always hot. This is good for roasted apples and pears. (A1393, 35)

CHAPTER TWO

Meatless Pottages

The pottages listed in this section are 'standard' pottages, the kind that would normally come at the beginning of a course of a dinner menu, but which could come almost anywhere. Most of them have the normal self-generated sauce to be expected of such a pottage. The first group consists of meatless pottages: those based primarily on almond milk, those based on nuts and flowers, egg-based meatless pottages, and others which are none of these; the second group is also generally meatless, but based on grains, vegetables, or fruit. Note that 'meatless' here does not preclude the possible use of meat-based broths.

Meatless pottages based on almond milk

Almond Milk Pottage

Make good almond milk of blanched almonds, thicker milk and thinner milk.[1] Put the thicker into a pot. Mix in grated white bread with the second milk; boil this on the fire. Colour it with saffron; sweeten it with honey, salt it, boil it, and add to the bread.[2] Give forth. (CCC, 24)

Amydon (Pudding)

Take amydon and boil it in good almond milk; add sugar to it. Arrange in dishes and then strew pomegranate seeds over it.[3] (DC, 60)

---

1. I.e., after straining the first batch, add more water to the used ground almonds to make a second, thinner, one. This recipe does not tell us what to do with the 'thicker' milk: presumably that is added at some point.
2. Perhaps this means bread sops? In any case, the recipe is confusingly phrased; what do we do with the 'thicker' milk?
3. Other recipes suggest other garnishes.

Caudle of Almonds

Take blanched almonds and draw them up with wine; add ground ginger and sugar, and colour it with saffron. Boil it, put a little salt on it, and serve it forth.[4] (FC, 90)

Charlet Coloured

Take blanched almonds and grind them and dilute them with red wine, and mix it with rice flour, and add pine nuts and spices; and colour it with saffron, and add sugar, and boil it and salt it, and serve it with anise in comfit. (NBC, 217)

A Cold Pottage

Take wine and draw a good thick milk of almonds with it, if you can; then put it in a pot and add to it ground cinnamon and ginger and saffron. Let it boil, and put it on a cloth, and if you wish let it be in different colours, one white without spices and the other yellow with spices. (H279 PD, 131)

Another Cold Pottage, Violet or Red

Take cream of almonds; mix it with sweet wine. Add a great deal of crushed white sugar; work it well with a saucer in a bowl, until it is as soft as you wish to have it.[5] Arrange it for serving in the manner of a Caudle Ferry. Decorate it with red anise in comfit. If you wish, you can change the colour of the pottage: take blue turnesole and wash it and wring it well in the wine that you had mixed with your cream, and if you wish you can take red turnesole and wash it and wring it in the same way and make it red. And you can strengthen it well with ground ginger. You can dress the white and that together in a dish in the manner of a very thick pudding, decorated with anise in comfit, the white with red anise and the red with white.

And, if you wish, you can make of it a cold baked dish, arranged in the same ways in pastry shells baked before. You can, where you wish, divide it into a cold pottage or a cold baked dish with all sorts of sauces made with fruits. You can take strawberries and hurtleberries and cherries; take out the

4.   Other recipes give ale as an alternative to wine. A recipe for 'Caudle Out of Lent' adds beaten eggs.
5.   The sugar would have been taken from a hard loaf.

stones and strew them in the pastry cases, and arrange your pottage above. Serve forth. That is a good service for supper. You may add cinnamon and sanders and other spice powders to make it brown. (RD12, 120)

Comyne

Make good almond milk and let it boil, and put in cumin and amydon; and colour it with saffron, and then serve it, and strew pomegranate seeds or raisins on it, if you have no other sugar. (DC, 59)

Cream, Coloured

Make thick almond milk and put it in a pot and boil it over the fire; then take a clean canvas and put it on this, and let the water run out. Take a half portion and put it in an earthen pot; then take the other half portion and divide it in two, and make half of it yellow, and add to it wine, sugar, cloves, mace, ground cinnamon. Take [*blank in MS*] and grind a little in a mortar; then mix it with almond milk, and do each of them in a pot, and see that they are equally thick, and set it over the fire and boil it little, and serve forth.[6] (H279 PD, 77)

Egredouce (Sweet and sour pottage)

Take almonds and make good milk, and mix it with good clean vinegar. Take raisins and boil them in clean water; take them out of the water and boil them with [the] milk, and if you wish colour it with saffron, and serve it forth.[7] (DS, 51)

Ermine

It is to be made white, and well seasoned with good ground ginger and cubebs and cloves, and served with Vertdesire.[8] (DC, 29)

---

6.   Obviously more than a word or two was left out. There is no other version of this recipe to check.
7.   Most versions of this dish call for meat or fish, usually accompanied by onions; what are indispensable are the sweet and sour ingredients.
8.   See below, page 107; apparently 'Ermine' is also a pottage based on almond milk.

Fauntemper

Take almond milk, rice flour, sugar, and good ground ginger, galingale, cinnamon; and take good herbs, crush them and grind them, putting them through a cloth, and add them, and boil it. Mix in yolks of eggs and boil it some more. Then take maces, cubebs, and cloves[9] and add when you arrange it for serving. (H279 PD70)

Godrich Stew

Grind raisins; draw them with sweet wine. Put in ground ginger and cinnamon, Lombard powder[10] and clarified sugar. Put it in a pot with cream of almonds; boil it up together. Stir it well when it begins to boil. Take it off; arrange it as a flat pottage. Decorate it with gilt cloves and serve forth. (RD12, 118)

Honey Douce (Pudding of almond milk and rice flour)

Take good milk of almonds and rice, and wash it [the rice] well in a clean container and in hot water, and afterwards put it in a towel to dry, and when it is dry grind it into flour in a mortar; then beat them [the rice flour and almond milk] together. Then take two parts, and put half in one pot and half in another, and colour one with saffron and let the other be white. Let it boil until it is thick, and add a good portion of sugar, then arrange it in two dishes. See that you have almonds boiled in water and in saffron and wine, and then fry them and set them upon this food, and strew sugar over it so that it is well coloured, and serve forth. (DS, 80)

Mortrews, Double (A pudding: not a true 'mortrews')

Almond milk, eggs, a portion of amydon, galingale, ginger, hard-boiled eggs chopped small and added, sugar, lozenges[11] scattered above; the colour is yellow. (DC, 8)

---

9. The word used here, *geloferys*, may mean gillyflowers, but probably means cloves: unlikely as those may seem as a last-minute addition.
10. A commercial mixture.
11. Noodles?

A Pottage

Boil a few eggs in red wine; then draw them through a strainer with good milk of almonds, and add to them currants, tailed dates, large raisins, pine nuts, ground pepper, sanders, cloves, maces, enough honey to make it a little sweet, and salt. Then bind it up flat with a little rice flour and make it red with sanders, and serve it in flat. And if you wish, in flesh time put chopped veal on it, but not too small. (H279 PD, 149)

Pourviens de Hay (An accompaniment to blancmanger)

Take sloes and grind them with all the stones. Take almonds and wash them in cold water; grind them, hulls and all. Mix them with cold water. Draw the milk and mix it with the ground sloes; mix it well together. Mix amydon ground with ale and put all this in a clean pot. Set it on the fire and stir it well. Add sugar and take off the fire.

When it is all cooked, put it in cold water, then set it on the fire again and boil it well; then take it off the fire and take sugar and as much of ground cinnamon, and mix them together, and arrange the pottage on the side of the dish with your spice powder on top. Take cloves and stick them on it, and afterwards arrange Blancmanger on the other side and serve it forth.[12] (RD12, 172)

Russntayles (Bread and dried fruit pudding)

Take almonds and grind them; mix them with wine or ale. Mince figs and raisins finely, and minced dates and good white bread minced as small as the dates: add them all. Colour it with saffron, and let it be very thick. Cut blanched almonds lengthwise and fry them in oil; make a garnish of them, with ground ginger and sugar, and put this on top. (RD12, 166)

Tanne (A spiced almond milk)

Take almond milk and sugar and ground ginger, and galingale and cinnamon and red wine, and boil it all together. That is good Tanne. (H279 PD, 111)

---

12.   The 'hay' in the title here is even more puzzling than that in CCC's 'Lampray Hay': at least we know lampreys were sometimes rubbed with hay.

Tayle (Dried fruit pudding)

Take a little milk of almonds drawn up with wine and put it in a pot; add figs, raisins, cut dates, and sugar and good spice powders. Boil it up; colour it with saffron and serve it forth.[13] (OP, 67)

Meatless pottages based on nuts and flowers

Acorn Pottage

Put almond milk in a pot. Take roasted acorn kernels; grind them, mix them with wine or ale. Add to this a large portion of sugar, sanders, saffron, and other seasonings, and season it up with spices; and take the shells and put them on top [as a garnish]. (OP, 71)

Chauden of the Wood (Hazelnut pottage)

Take small nut kernels as you do of almonds and fry them in oil; then boil them in almond milk. Add cloves, mace, and pine nuts. Fry nut kernels and colour them with saffron and serve them.[14] (NBC, 260)

Fawne (Bean blossom pottage)

Take the leaves and blossoms of beans and grind them, and mix them with the broth of fresh beef or of chickens, and add crumbled wastel bread so that it will be thick, and salt it; add sugar and saffron and arrange it in dishes, and decorate them with bean blossoms, and serve it forth. (UC, 36)

Hazelnuts in Season (Hazelnut pottage)

Almond milk, rice flour, the [nut] kernels fried; choice ginger, sugar to balance the bitterness, nuts set on top.(AN B, 10)

Heppee (Rose hip pottage)

Take rose hips and pick out the stones and the ridges around them, and

13.   This recipe forgets the bread; some others substitute rice flour. That in H5401, 69 includes bread but does not add any fruits.

14.   Another recipe, LCC, 55, recommends thickening the pottage with rice flour and makes it clear that the additional fried nuts are to decorate the dish.

wash them and grind them; and take the broth of fresh beef, or of chickens, and mix them with this, and boil them. And salt them, and add sugar, and dress it in dishes, and put the rose flowers above, and serve it forth in a mannerly way. (UC, 37)

Primrose Pottage

Take primrose petals and grind them in a mortar, and mix them with almond milk or good cow's milk, and thicken it with boiling minced bread, and salt it. And add sugar and saffron, and make it thick; arrange it for serving. Strew primrose flowers on top, and serve it forth.[15] (UC, 34)

Rosee

Take a handful of rose petals or two and grind them well in a mortar, and then mix them with almond milk or cow's milk; put in a little bread and mix well with spices and eggs coloured with saffron, and case a petal or two over it, and then serve.[16] (DC, 36)

Spinee (Hawthorn blossom pottage)

Take cleanly gathered hawthorn blossoms and grind them to a powder in a mortar; mix with almond or cow's milk, then thicken with bread or amydon, and with eggs, and decorate it with hawthorn blossoms and elder blossoms. (AN B, 15)

Suade (Elderflower pottage)

Almond's milk, amydon, thickened with elderflowers; the flowers shall be washed and put in plenty of ginger, with elderflowers strewn above. The colour shall be white. (DC, 23)

Violet Pottage

Take violet flowers and grind them, and take minced white bread and add it, and mix it with almond milk or cow's milk, and add sugar and boil it, and salt it, and arrange it and Primrose Pottage together, and strew violet flowers over it as you do its flowers on the Primrose Pottage. (UC, 35)

15.   'Primrose Pottage at Easter' is almost identical.
16.   Some recipes put in ground meat, usually chicken.

Meatless pottages based on eggs

Caudle

Take eggs and beat them well together; heat ale and add to them. Add amydon and a portion of sugar, or a part of honey, and a part of saffron; Boil it and give it forth.[17] (L553, 9)

Caudle Ferry

Take raw egg yolks, separated from the whites; then take good wine and warm in a pot on a good fire, and put in the yolks and stir it well, but do not let it boil until it becomes thick. Add sugar, saffron and salt, maces, cloves, and ground galingale and cinnamon, and when you serve it sprinkle white powder on it.[18] (H279 PD, 47)

Jussel (Broth with eggs and bread)

Take grated bread and eggs and beat them together; add saffron, sage, and salt, and mix it with broth. Boil it and serve it forth.[19] (FC, 44)

Tredure

Take bread and grate it; make a thickening of raw eggs, and add saffron and mild spice powder, and mix it with good broth and make it like a caudle. Add to it a little verjuice. (FC, 17)

---

17.   Other recipes suggest wine as an alternative to ale, and/or ask for yolks only.
18.   The recipe for 'White Powder' is given on page 22, above. The main difference between 'Caudle Ferry' and plain 'caudle' (sometimes entitled 'Thin Caudle') seems to be that the wine for Caudle Ferry is heated beforehand; sometimes another thickener, such as flour, is added, so that it is indeed thicker than the 'Thin Caudle'.
19.   The eggs and bread are intended to form a curd, not to act as a thickener. Fish versions use the roe in place of eggs, and 'Jussel with Sauce' is served in a sort of cream sauce rather than the original broth.

Other meatless pottages

Cressadys

Take sugar, bastard wine,[20] and amydon, and mix them all together. Season it with vinegar and ground grains of paradise, and colour it with turnesole, and add salt (S7 17)

Payn Fondue ('Drowned bread')

Take bread; fry it in grease or oil. Put it in red wine and grind it with raisins, and draw it up. Clarify honey with white of eggs and water; skim it clean and mix it in. Add cloves, maces, minced ginger, good spice powder, and salt. Make sure it is very thick, and decorate it with anise in comfit. (OP, 82)

20. A sweet wine.

CHAPTER THREE

Pottages Based on Grains, Vegetables or Fruit

Grains

Rice

Take a portion of rice and pick them clean, and boil them well, and let them cool; then take good milk of almonds and add it, and cook and stir it well; and add sugar and honey and serve forth.[1] (H279 PD, 86)

Rice Lombard

Take rice and pick them clean and wash them, and parboil them, and put them in a pot; add good beef broth and sugar or honey and let it boil, and colour it with saffron; and if you want to have it very thick, take raw egg yolks and beat them well together, and draw them through a strainer, and put it in the pot and let it boil with the pottage, and then arrange it in dishes and take hard egg yolks and cloves and maces and minced ginger, and mix them together, and strew on top, and serve it forth. (Ar 334, 63)

Rysmole (Pottage of ground rice)

Take rice and grind it very well in a mortar, and add good almond milk and sugar and salt; boil it and serve it forth. (DS, 64)

Frumenty (Wheat pottage)

Take wheat and pick it over well, and pound it in a mortar and sprinkle it with water, and pound it to remove the hulls. Wash it well and put it in a pot. Boil it until it bursts; set it down. Take cow's milk and stir it together

---

1. Some recipes call for broth rather than almond milk, and some offer a choice between broth, for a meat day, or almond milk; FC, 11 has it both ways: cooking the rice in meat broth and then mixing it with almond milk. 'Rice Cameline' (P, 10) seasons rice in almond milk with cinnamon, while NBC, 231's 'Rice' grinds up the rice and turns it into a sort of pudding.

until it is thick; mix it up with yolks of eggs. Colour it with saffron. Stir it well.[2] (GK, [Royal 8.B.iv] 2)

Vegetables

Aquapatys

Peel garlic and put it in a pot with water and oil and boil it. Add to it saffron, salt, and strong spice powder, and serve it hot. (FC, 77)

Bean Pottage (1)

Take dried beans, and if you wish to soak them a little, and mix them up with almond milk. Add sugar and salt to this. Out of Lent, make them up with cow's milk, and add sugar and salt and clarified butter. (OP, 3)

Bean Pottage (2)

Take [dried] white beans and boil them in water, and grind the beans thoroughly in a mortar, and boil them in almond milk, and add to this wine and honey; and boil raisins in wine and add them to this, and then serve it forth. (DS, 81)

Beans, Drawn

Take [dried] beans and boil them, and grind them in a mortar, and mix them with good broth; and put chopped onions in the broth and colour it with saffron, and serve it forth.[3] (FC, 4)

Beans, Dried, with Bacon

Take beans and dry them in a kiln or in an oven. Hull them well, and discard the hulls, and wash them clean; and put them to boil in good broth, and eat them with bacon. (FC, 3)

---

2. Recipes headed 'Venison with Frumenty' may add, 'And your venison in another dish'. Frumenty to be served with porpoise is made the same way, but with almond milk substituted for cow's milk and eggs.
3. 'Makke' (FC, 76) is similar: the ground boiled beans are mixed with red wine, then served with fried minced onions.

Beans, Fried

Take beans and boil them until they almost burst, then wring out all the water. Add to them fried onions minced with garlic; fry them in oil or grease, and add mild spice powder[4] and serve it forth. (FC, 189)

Cabbages

Take good cabbages; pick them over and wash them and parboil them, then press out the water on a clean board, chop them, and put them in a clean pot with good fresh broth and marrow bones. Let them boil. Then take good grated bread and add that, and saffron and salt, and let it boil enough. Then serve it forth.[5] (H4016, 3)

Chebolace (Scallions, spring onions)

Take onions and herbs and chop them small, and add to them good broth; and treat it as you did cabbages. If it is a fish day, make in the same way with water and oil, and if it is not in Lent, mix in yolks of eggs, and serve it forth; and put in mild spice powder. (FC, 9)

Chickpeas

Take chickpeas and cover them in ashes[6] all night or all day, or lay them in hot embers. In the morning wash them in clean water and put them over the fire in clean water. Boil them and put in oil, whole garlic, saffron, strong spices,[7] and salt; boil it and serve it forth. (FC, 73)

Fennel, Sops in

Take blades of fennel; shred them, but not too finely. Put them to boil in water and oil, with minced onions; add saffron and salt and mild spice powder. Serve it forth. Take toasted bread and pour the soup over it. (FC, 79)

---

4. 'White powder' may be meant: see recipe on page 22, above.
5. Most of the other cabbage recipes are very close to this one; two add onions and leeks, and one calls for blanching the cabbage and stripping off the outside layer
6. I.e., under or beside a low fire.
7. 'Pouder fort'.

Joutes (Pottage of chopped pot herbs)

Take borage, cabbage, langdebef, parsley, beet greens, orage, avens, violets, savory, and fennel, and when they are boiled press out the water and chop them small; put them in good broth and boil them and serve them forth.[8] (FC, 8)

Joutes, French

Take white peas and boil them, and purée them; and parboil herbs and chop them in large pieces, and put them in a pot with the purée. Peel onions and boil them well whole in water, and add them to the purée with oil and salt; colour it with saffron and serve it, and sprinkle on it mild spice powder.[9] (FC, 75)

Kale

Take fresh mutton, or veal or pork, broth; chop your greens and parsley small, and when it boils put them in. Put some groats among your greens and boil them along with it. If you have salt meat cooking, take a piece out of the pot to cook by itself, then take it up and put in your greens. In the meantime, you will get good gravy to season your greens when off the heat.[10] (LCC, 107)

Lupins

Take lupins and parboil them; take off the hulls with pounding [in a mortar] and boil them in fish broth. Add to them sugar, salt, saffron, and ground ginger, and serve it forth. (FC, 74)

Mushrooms (Boiled with leeks)

Take mushrooms and pare them clean, and dice them; take leeks and shred them small, and put them to boil in good broth. Colour it with saffron, and put in strong spice powder. (FC, 12)

8. Some recipes add further meat, such as marrowbones, and/or a bread thickening; many advise serving this with a dish of bacon. One early recipe entitled 'Joutes Endored' (DC, 47) adds pork fat and saffron. Most fish-day versions substitute almond milk for broth.
9. OP labels a similar dish, with almond milk and fried raisins added, 'Long Worts', and another, without the peas but with onions, almond milk, etc., 'Lenten Greens'.
10. A second kale recipe in this collection is very simple: boil it in water, press out the water, and season with butter.

Mushrooms Flourished

First, you shall make them very clean. Put cold lard in cold water, and then cut it up. Take the mushrooms and lard them carefully with the pieces of lard, and then roast them. When they have roasted enough, [baste with] eggs without the whites, and on the griddle flourish with spices, using mixed cloves and cinnamon. (DC, 55)

Peas of Almayne (German peas)

Take white peas and wash them, and boil them a good while; then wash them in cold water until the hulls are all off. Put them in a pot and cover it well so that no breath passes out, and boil them very well; and put in good almond milk and a portion of rice flour and salt and saffron, and serve it forth. (DS, 2)

Peas, Dried with Bacon

Take dried peas and boil them in meat broth with bacon; then hull them and grind half of them in a mortar, mixed with the broth, and strain them, and put them back in the pot and let them boil until they thicken themselves; and serve it forth.[11] (Ar 334, 165)

Peas, Green

Take young green peas and boil them with good beef broth, and take parsley, sage, savory, hyssop, and a little bread and bray all that together in a mortar with some of the peas; mix this with the broth and put it in the pot with the rest of the peas and let it boil together, and serve it forth.[12] (Ar 334, 11)

Peas, White in Gravy

Take white [dried] peas and hull them in the way one does cabbages or leeks; then boil them with almond milk, put enough sugar in, and fried onions and oil, and serve. (H279 PD, 148)

11. The LCC recipe for 'grey' peas advises soaking them overnight and hulling them before boiling.
12. The next recipe advises, instead of straining part of the peas with the added herbs, cooking it all together until it 'thickens' itself. Another (later) Ar 334 recipe for 'Green Peas Royal' advises adding almond milk to the ground portion of peas and herbs and finally thickening it with eggs.

Porre

Take green or white peas, washed clean, and boil them, and set them on the side until the broth runs clear, and run that same clear broth through a strainer into a pot, and to it add parsley, chopped sage, minced onions, and ground pepper, and colour it deeply with saffron. And add a little wine to it, and let it boil; and when you take it off the fire, add a little vinegar. And take pieces of bread toasted, and put them in the same pot when taking it up, and serve forth.[13] (Ar 334, 186)

Porre Chaplain (Onion soup with pastry rings)

Take a hundred onions, or half that many, and take olive oil and boil them together in a pot; and take almond milk, and boil it, and add it. Make a thin pastry of dough, and make rings out of it; fry them in olive oil or white grease, and boil all together. (DS, 88)

Porre of Cabbages

Lay them [the cabbages] overnight in a running stream of water, and in the morning set water on the fire, and when the water is scalding hot, throw them in; and hull them in the same way as other porre,[14] and serve forth. (H279 PD, 146)

Porre of Split Peas

Set peas on the fire; boil them tender, then grind them in a mortar, push them through a strainer. Pick out any that are soiled. Then put it in a pot and add onions and parsley. Sweeten it with honey, colour it with saffron, and add ground pepper to it. Then take a loaf diced small; fry this bread in a little oil, so that the bread absorbs the oil. Then put all this in a pot and boil it, and serve it forth. (CCC, 39)

13.   Some recipes, entitled 'Porre of Peas', are simpler than this, but they make it clear that the peas themselves, not just the broth, are strained – as no doubt they should be here; almond milk and rice flour are added in some cases. Those for 'Porre of White Peas' call for almond milk and dried fruits.

14.   The recipe here refers to a preceding one that gives a rather complex method of hulling peas.

Porre, White (Porre of leeks)

Take white of leeks and parboil them, and chop them small with onions. Add good broth and boil it up with small birds. Colour it with saffron and season it with mild spice powder.[15] (FC, 2)

Spinach, Fried

Take spinach and parboil it in boiling water. Take it up and press out the water and cut it in two. Fry it in oil, and add mild spice powder, and serve forth. (FC, 188)

Turnips in Pottage

Take turnips and make them clean, and wash them clean; quarter them and parboil them, then take them up, put them in a good broth and boil them. Mince onions, and add saffron and salt, and serve it forth with mild spice powder; treat pasturnaks and skirrets [other root vegetables] in the same way. (FC, 7)

Worts (Greens)

To make greens, take greens and strip them from the stalks; beet greens, borage, avens, violets, mallows, parsley, bettany, primrose, patience, the white of leeks, and crops of nettles. Parboil them and press out the water on a board, chop them small, and add oatmeal to them. Take broth of conger, turbot, salmon, or other good fish, and put it in the pot with the herbs. When the pot comes to a boil add the greens and boil them and salt them.

And if you lack broth, take eels and boil them; then take them out and strip the fish from the bone and add it to the broth, and put in the greens and cook them. You can also wash mussels and boil them; put in as much water as they could swim in, and boil them until they open. Strain the broth, and take some herbs as you did before and add them to the mussel broth; then set them on the fire and boil it, and when they are almost boiled add your cooked mussels and salt them.

And you can strain some cooked [dried] peas and cook them with the

15.   This is the only recipe that calls for adding 'small birds'; others call for eels or no such addition. Some call for almond milk, and/or other thickeners.

greens. Add fresh water and clear oil that has been fried; in boiling it, thicken with the peas, and do not put in any oatmeal. And you can parboil the white of leeks, press out the water and chop them small. Then take dried beans with fresh water and boil them; add the white of leeks, but do not add any oatmeal; salt it and serve it. (NBC, 167)

Worts, Buttered

Take all the kinds of good herbs that you can get, and do with them as said above; put them on the fire with good water. Add a great quantity of clarified butter; when they are boiled enough, salt them, but put no oatmeal in. Dice bread small and arrange in dishes and pour on the greens, and serve them forth. (H4016, 2)

Worts, Long

Take greens; strip off the leaves and parboil them in water. Then take them and press them, then cut them so that every blade is an inch long. Put these greens into a pot with fresh broth of beef and mutton and capons: be sure that the broth is rich. Then fry bread in grease; put this bread into the pot. When it is time to go to dine, add saffron and salt and give forth.[16] (CCC, 61)

Worts, White

Select herbs as you did for Joutes [above], and boil them in water until they are soft; then take them up and pound them on a board as dry as you can. Then chop them small and put them in a pot and mix them with rice flour. Take almond milk and add it, and honey, but not too much so that it won't be too sweet, and saffron and salt; and serve it forth, for a proper good pottage.[17] (H279, 5)

16. Meat-free versions generally omit the bread and add the greens, with onions, to a pea purée, then fry them; or add fish broth.
17. OP's 'Lenten Greens' omits the rice flour, calls for sugar rather than honey, and adds onions and fried raisins.

Fruit

Applemoys (Enriched apple sauce)

Take apples and boil them in water; push them through a strainer. Add almond milk and honey and rice flour, saffron and strong spice powder and salt, and boil it until it is thick.[18] (FC, 81)

Aturmyn

Take rice; pick it, wash it, boil it on the fire. Then boil figs in wine or in ale; grind them, mix them with wine or ale. Then mix this completed syrup with the drained rice, and good clarified honey. Put into it currants or cut dates and also a few maces, ground pepper and sanders. Half a pound of rice and one pound of figs is enough for eight dishes. (CCC, 40)

Bullace Plums

Take bullace plums and scald them with wine, and draw them through a strainer; put them in a pot. Clarify honey and add it to this, along with strong spice powder and rice flour. Salt it and decorate it with white anise in comfit, and serve it forth.[19] (FC, 98)

Cherry Pottage

Take cherries and discard the stones and grind them well, and draw them through a strainer, and put in a pot. Add to this white grease or sweet butter and ground white bread, and put in good wine and sugar, and salt it, and stir it well together, and arrange it in dishes; and decorate with cloves and strew sugar on top.[20] (UC, 33)

Cherries, Stuffed

Take away the stone with all the tail, and then make a stuffing of fresh things [cherries?] and of hen's flesh beaten in a mortar. Mix with hard

18. A few versions, such as DS, 63, are somewhat simpler, but 'Apples Royal' (H279, 135) is a further enriched and elaborated version.
19. A more elaborate version calls for serving this as a basis for stewed pears and stuffed dates, and one called 'Lorey of Bullace Plums' uses a thickening of bread crumbs and egg yolks.
20. Some recipes add almond milk, and at least one (DC, 14) adds meat.

yolks, and soft yolks to hold it well together, and pepper, cinnamon, and cloves. The cherries, well stuffed, put in a pail, with stuffing all around them. Then put it in a silver dish and bear the dish to the dais before all men. (UC, 54)

Cold Leach Food (Cold fruit slices)

Take quinces and pare them. Core them and cut them into small pieces, and put them in an earthen pot, and add white grease mixed with clarified honey and raw egg yolks and a little almond milk. Add powdered saffron, and slice it to serve. (NBC, 65)

Figgy Pottage

Take figs and boil them in wine, and grind them in a mortar with bread crumbs. Mix it with good wine; boil it. Add good spices and whole raisins; arrange it and decorate it with pomegranate seeds.[21] (DS, 62)

Fruit Pottage

Take figs and raisins and remove the seeds, and a good part of apples, and discard the parings and the seeds; grind them well in a mortar and mix them with almond milk and with rice flour, so that it will be well thickened. Strew ground galingale on it, and serve it forth. (DS, 83)

Garnade (Pomegranate pudding)

Take almond milk made with vernage[22] and add to it sugar and coarsely minced ginger, and let it boil well so that it is very thick, and if it is not thick enough take rice flour or capon's meat ground in a mortar. And take boiled rice, and mix it with pomegranate juice, and add it to the pot and stir it together well. And add rosewater, and colour it with [red] turnesole, and serve it. (NBC, 29)

21. Some recipes add honey.
22. A strong, sweet Italian wine

Haslets on Fish Day

Take quartered figs, whole raisins and whole dates and almonds. Run them on a spit and roast them, and endore them as you would Golden Meatballs,[23] and serve them forth.[24] (FC, 195)

Macaroon (A dish of ground dates and currants) [25]

Lay dates in white wine all night long, and in the morning grind them small and smooth in a mortar. Season them with enough ground cinnamon, ground cloves, and mace, and mix them with currants; add ground pepper and salt, and serve it forth.[26] (Sl 7, 20)

Pearmoys (Mashed pears)

Take pears pared clean. Grind them finely and draw them through a strainer with raw cream, in as stiff a mixture as you can make it. Season it with ground ginger and add sanders mixed with wine and sugar, and serve it forth. (eM, 30)

Pears in Comfit

Take pears and pare them clean. Take good red wine and mulberries, or sanders, and boil the pears in this, and when they are done take them up. Make a sauce of Greek [sweet] wine, or vernage, with white powder[27] or white sugar and ground ginger, and put the pears in this. Cook it a little and serve it forth. (FC, 136)

---

23. See 'Farsure', Stuffing, on page 18, above, for the recipe for those 'Golden Meatballs'.
24. 'Haslets' were originally spit-roasted pieces of meat, but all recipes extant are for fish-day substitutes, including one jokingly entitled 'Lampray Hay' (see recipe, CCC, 22, for explanation).
25. Clearly, of no visible relationship to the dish of that name today.
26. 'Mesegew' (eM, 33), a similar dish, calls for grinding the dates before adding wine, seasoning with cinnamon and vinegar, and adding chopped minced almonds rather than currants; 'Message' (Sl 7, 18) mixes the ground dates with minced pears and white wine.
27. See recipe on page 22, above.

Pears in Compost (Preserved pears) [28]

Take wine and cinnamon and a great deal of white sugar and set it on the fire, and heat it until it is hot, but do not let it boil, and draw it through a strainer. Then take good dates and pick out the stones, and slice them very thin, and add them; then take wardon pears and pare them and boil them, and slice them thin, and add them to the sauce. Then take a little sanders and add that, and set it on the fire; and if you have any chardequince, add that to what is boiling, and make sure it has enough sugar and is well seasoned with cinnamon, and add salt and let it boil; and then put it in a wooden container and let it cool, and serve it forth. (H279 PD, 35)

Pears in Rampant Perre

Pears boiled in water, thickened with eggs and with amydon, with the leaves strewn above; make of dough, coloured yellow, three rampant lions in the dishes. (DC, 24)

Pears in Syrup

Take wardon pears and put them in a pot and boil them until they are tender; then take them up and pare them, and cut them into pieces. Take enough ground cinnamon, a good quantity, and put it in red wine, and draw it through a strainer; add sugar to it and put it in an earthen pot, and let it boil, and then add the pears to it. Let it boil together, and when they have boiled a while take ground ginger and add it, and a little vinegar and a little saffron; and see that it is poignant and sweet.[29] (H279, 10)

Plums, White

A serving of white plums is rich and precious. Take plums and remove the stones, and then boil them in water; then take them out of the crock and chop them well with eggs. Mix this in a pail, stirring it well; then take fresh grease, pepper and cinnamon, and mix them in. When it is cooked and well turned over, then is the serving brought forth. (DC, 49)

28. This is a lightly 'preserved' version, not for lengthy keeping like the 'Preserved Pears' in the preliminary section (Chapter 1, above).
29. A formula designating the desired sweet and sour taste.

A Pottage on a Fish Day

Boil two or three pared apples and strain them through a strainer with rice flour; then take the white wine it was cooked in and strain it, and see it is not too bound with rice flour if it boils, and add sanders and saffron, so that the colours are marbled. Then take currants and add them, and put enough shredded almonds on it; and mince dates small and put them on it, and a little honey to make it sweet, or else sugar. Then add maces and cloves, pepper, cinnamon, ginger, and enough other spices; then take pears and boil them a little, then rake them on the coals until they are tender; then shred them in small round pieces, and a little before you serve it put them on the pottage, and so serve it in almost flat, but not fully so. (H279 PD, 129)

Pottage Royal (A fig-based pottage)

Grind figs dry, with a little moisture of osay; draw them up as well as two strong men can draw it, then separate the mixture into two parts. Mix up the first part as thick as mortrews,[30] and add to it cinnamon, ground ginger, a little vinegar, and salt. (S7 11)

Quinade (Stewed quinces)

Take quinces and pare them. Pick out the best and put them in an earthen pot; add white grease, so that they will stew in it, and mix in clarified honey and raw egg yolks, with a little almond milk. And put in strong spice powder and saffron, and see that it can be sliced. (FC, 20)

Raisins on Fish Days

Take almonds and wash them clean and grind them, and draw them up with fresh water. Boil it, and put raisins in it; add salt, saffron, and sugar, and put coriander on it and serve. (H5401, 79)

---

30.   Using more osay. (Osay, or ossey, ozey. A sweet French wine, *vin d'Aussay,* wine of Alsace.)

Rapee

Take half figs and half raisins; pick them over and wash them in water. Scald them in wine, grind them in a mortar, and push them through a strainer. Put them in a pot with ground pepper and other good spice powders; mix in rice flour and colour it with sanders. Salt it, boil, it, and serve it forth.[31] (FC, 85)

Strawberry Pottage

Gather strawberries cleanly and grind them; take almond or cow's milk and mix thoroughly, then add a little bread and some eggs, and thicken the mixture well. Colour it with saffron and put whole strawberries on top.[32] (AN A, 17)

31. Some of the recipes of this title resemble this one, others do not. Some consist mainly of fish with a bread thickener: 'Rapee of Fish' (NBC, 264) has a sauce of bread ground with raisins and cinnamon; 'Rapee Bastard' (RD12, 117) differs from this one mainly in containing almond milk and honey and 'Rapee Royal' (OP, A.5) is similar; 'Rapee of Meat' contains pork, egg yolks, and honey; 'Rapee, Myles in' is a dish of fried meatballs of ground fruit, fish, and boiled eggs – and the many dishes simply entitled 'Rapee' are almost as various, with no feature obviously in common.

32. Some versions add meat to the pottage, and most add seasonings: H279's recipe is very spicy.

CHAPTER FOUR

Meat- and Fish-based Pottages

Meat-based

Amyn of Meat

Boil capons. Take the flesh from the bones; chop it and grind it. Take good almond milk drawn with the capon broth and mix up the meat therewith. Grind the bones; mix them into it with some of the broth. Colour it with saffron. Put in maces, cloves, cubebs and spice powders and sugar; add flour of rice so that it is very thick, and serve forth.[1] (RD12, 24)

Anesere

Almond milk, rice flour, capon meat, blanched almonds fried and mixed in and fried almonds inserted on top; the colour, yellow with saffron.[2] (DC, 3)

Bardolf

Make a thick almond milk with vernage[3] and let it boil, and put in ground capon meat, adding sugar, cloves, maces, pine nuts, and minced ginger. And take chickens, parboiled and chopped, and pull off the skin, and boil all of this together. In taking it off the fire add a little vinegar mixed with ground ginger and a little rosewater, and make the pottage thick, and serve it forth. (Ar 334, 180)

---

1. The fish version substitutes haddock, bream, pike, tench, and perch for the capon.
2. The name means it is yellow: this is a yellow version of Blancdesire, below. 'Spanish Dish' (DC, 4) is the same dish, substituting pistachios for almonds.
3. A strong, sweet Italian wine.

Berandyles

Take chickens and boil them with good beef; when they are tender take out the chickens and discard the bones and grind the meat finely in a mortar. Mix it with the broth and push it through a colander, and add to it ground ginger and sugar and pomegranate seeds, and boil it, and arrange it in dishes, and scatter on top cloves and maces and good ground spices, and serve it forth. (DC, 27)

Small Birds, Stewed

Take small birds and pluck them and draw them clean, and wash them well, and chop off the legs, and fry them well in a pan of fresh grease; then lay them on a clean linen cloth and let the grease run out. Then take onions, mince them small and fry them in clean fresh grease and put them in an earthen pot. Then mix a good portion of cinnamon and wine and draw it through a strainer, and put in the pot with the onions; add cloves and maces and a little ground pepper to this and let them boil together enough. Then add white sugar and ground ginger and saffron, and serve it forth.[4] (H279 PD, 19)

Blancdesire

Take blanched almonds; grind them and mix them with white wine, on a flesh day with broth, and put in rice flour or amydon, and mix that in. Add ground chicken, sugar, and salt, and decorate it with white anise in comfit. Put in saffron through a colander, and serve it forth.[5] (FC, 39)

Blanche Doucet (Sweet white dish)

Take capon meat, ground and blended with wine, and put it in a pot with a little honey or sugar; mix it with almonds and ground ginger, and put on top yolks of eggs. On fish days take perch, pike, or haddock, or other good

---

4.   No doubt with the birds.
5.   Other versions omit saffron (logically, for a 'white' dish). Some recipes call for fish on a fish day, but one meatless version calls for toasted almonds rather than chicken and there are also meatless, non-Lenten, versions using boiled eggs. Alternative garnishes include pomegranate seeds, red anise in comfit, and white (spice) powder.

fish; deal with it in the same way, and make pellets of paste to put on it as you did yolks of eggs on the meat-day version. (OP, 70)

Blancmanger

Take two parts of rice to a third part of almonds; wash the rice clean in lukewarm water and turn and boil it until the grains break, then let it cool. Take the [almond] milk and add it to the rice, and let them boil together, and add to this white grease and chicken meat ground small, and stir it well, and salt it, and arrange it in dishes. Fry almonds in fresh grease until they are brown, and put them on the dishes, and strew sugar on top, and serve forth.[6] (UC, 28)

Bours

Take lungs, hearts, ears, spleens, and ribs of a swine, or else take duck or goose, and chop them small, then parboil them in clean water; and then take them up and pick it clean into a good pot. Add to it enough ale, and sage and salt, and then boil it very well. Serve it forth for a good pottage.[7] (H279 PD, 15)

Brawn de Vine

A standing [i.e., very thick] pottage. Take good almond milk drawn up with fresh broth and put it in a pot. Grind fresh pork and chicken meat and put it in this. Put it on the fire, boil it, and add to it rice flour. Take the juice of vine leaves and parsley, with saffron, and add to it, and see that it has a deep green colour. Add to it sugar, salt, ground ginger and ground cinnamon, and put in grapes, and serve it forth. (P, 105)

Brawn in Pepper Sauce

Take wine and ground cinnamon and draw it through a strainer and set it on the fire, and let it boil, and add to it cloves, maces, and ground pepper.

6. One variant of this, 'Blancmanger Mole', calls for grinding the rice into rice flour and adding amydon, and another, 'Blancmanger Gros', calls for using chunks of the chicken instead of ground meat. One 'Blancmanger of Fish' recipe calls for perch or lobster; others call for a variety of white fish.
7. At least one later recipe calls for both pork and goose.

Then take small whole onions and parboil them in hot water, and add them, and let them boil together. Then take brawn [boar's meat or pork] and slice it, but not too thin; and if it is pickled, let it steep a while in hot water until it is tender, then add it to the sauce. Then take sanders and vinegar and add them, and thus serve forth; but do not let it be too thick or too thin, but as a pottage should be.[8] (H279 PD, 31)

Doucet Brawn (Sweet brawn)

Take fresh veal broth and add good spices and sugar and saffron. Have brawn [boar or pork] diced small, and when your sauce boils add the brawn to it. Serve forth. (RD12, 81)

Brawn in Peverade (Pork in pepper sauce)

Take wine and ground cinnamon and draw this through a strainer, and set in on the fire and let it boil, and add to it cloves, maces, and ground pepper; then take small whole onions and parboil them in hot water, and add them, and let it all boil together. Then take pork[9] and slice it, not too thin. And if it is pickled, let it steep a while in hot water until it is tender, then add it to the sauce; then take sanders and vinegar and add them, and let it boil all together until it is done. Then take ginger and add that, and so serve it forth; but let it be neither too thick nor too thin, but just as a pottage should be.[10] (H279 PD, 31)

Bruce

Take the white of leeks; slit them and shred them small. Take pigs' offal and parboil it in broth and wine, then take it up and put the leeks in the broth; boil, and add the offal. Make a thickening of bread, blood, and vinegar, and add to this strong spice powder;[11] boil onions and mince them and add them to this [pottage]. Treat porpoise in the same way. (FC, 13)

---

8. Another recipe calls for first cooking the brawn in chicken or beef broth.
9. Brawn: boar's meat may be intended; it is more likely to be pickled than pork.
10. None of the recipes for this dish seem to emphasize the pepper, as the title suggests should be the case.
11. 'Powder fort', which probably included pepper.

Bukkenade *see* **Veal in Bukkenade** (Chapter 6, below)

Capons *see* **Pheasants**

Carpusselles

Take sliced pork roasted on a gridiron and put it in a pot, and add wine, vinegar, sugar, and spices. Colour it with alkenet; when it is boiled, colour it and serve forth. (RD12, 18)

Caudle in Chicken Broth

Take good capon broth and white bread and stew it as if making a sauce; colour it well with saffron, and when the sauce is boiled set it off the fire. Then take a good portion of egg yolks and strain them, and let the eggs run into the sauce, and stir it well until it is smooth and not too thick, and then take the fat of the capon broth or of a leg of pork and add it, and serve it forth. (H5401, 30)

Caudle Ferry to Serve with Blancmanger

Take meat of capon or pork and chop it small, and put it in a mortar and grind it well, and mix it with capon broth so that it is quite thick; then take almond milk, egg yolks, and saffron, and blend them all together so that it is yellow, and add ground cinnamon, and stick cloves on it, maces, and cubebs, and serve forth. (H279 PD, 139)

Cayce

Take ginger, cinnamon, galingale, and cloves and grind them together. Take a scalded pig and chickens or other fresh meat; chop it in small morsels and boil it in wine. Add to it parsley and sage and some unground saffron. Let it stand until it is cold.[12] (RD12, 178)

12.   The recipe entitled 'Celse' in WW, 57 appears to be the same recipe, but substituting a thickener for the herbs and directing us to 'dry' it rather than serve cold; but 'dry' may mean 'serve cold'. I do not know what either title means, so cannot say which is likely to be correct.

Charlet

Take pork and boil it well, and chop it small. Take eggs with all the whites and beat them well together, and add good sweet [cow's] milk to it, and boil it and serve it forth.[13] (DS, 20)

Charmerchand

Take ribs of mutton chopped and put them in a clean pot and set it on the fire with clean water, and boil it well. And then take parsley and sage and grind them in a mortar with bread, and mix this with the broth, and put it in the pot with the fresh meat and let it boil well together; and salt it and serve it. (NBC, 3)

Chauden Pottage

Take the liver and the lungs of the hart, and the midriff and the guts, and rub them with salt and boil them all together, and chop them small; and take bread and pepper and grind them together, and mix it with the broth, and colour it with the blood, and chop the chauden and put it in, and thicken it with egg yolks; and if you put lean meat in, colour it with saffron. (UC, 6)

Chicken in Civy (Chicken in onion sauce)

Scald chickens; draw them, chop them raw, [each] chicken into four or seven [pieces]; put them in a pot. If you have fresh broth of other meat, add some, skimmed of fat, or else add to it a leg of fresh beef. Add minced onions and herbs, and also pepper and cloves, maces and sanders. Then grind together crusts of bread with a few figs; mix them with wine. Boil the chickens well until tender; then add this liquid to them. If it is too thick, dilute it with wine. Arrange it in dishes; sprinkle with ground ginger and cinnamon, and give forth. (CCC, 66)

13.   The fish-day versions call for fish cooked in almond milk; recipes for charlet in a sauce advise a simple sauce of cow's milk thickened with eggs or thick almond milk, spiced, to be poured over slices of charlet which have been pressed down to remove excess fluid.

Chicken Compot

Take chickens and cut them in small pieces. Then take sage, parsley, leeks, and other herbs and wash them and break them with your hands. Then take a pint of honey and some of the herbs and put them in a pot and add the chicken to this, along with a little pork or pork fat minced, ground ginger and cinnamon, and a little wine. Cover the pot and cook it and serve it.[14] (NBC, 238)

Chicken in Concys

Take capons and roast them over a hot fire until they are half done, and chop them into gobbets and put them in a pot; add fresh broth. Boil them until they are tender. Take bread and this same broth and mix them together; add strong spices and saffron and salt. Take eggs and boil them until hard; take out the yolks and chop the whites. Take the pot from the fire and put the whites in it. Arrange this in dishes, and on top lay the yolks, whole, and decorate it with cloves.[15] (FC, 24)

Chicken in Dubatte (Braised chicken)

Take a chicken and roast it until almost done, and chop it in good pieces, and put it in a pot. Add to it fresh broth and half wine, cloves, maces, pepper, and cinnamon, and steep it in its own broth, fresh broth, and vinegar; and when it is done, serve it forth. (H279 PD, 41)

Chicken in Gauncele (Chicken in yellow garlic sauce)

Take chickens and roast them. Take milk and ground garlic and put it in a pan, and chop your chickens into this with yolks of eggs, and colour it with saffron and milk, and serve forth. (H279 PD, 90)

14. The name of this dish derives from the honey: a 'compost' (< Fr. *composte, compote*) was usually something preserved in honey, but of course this is not a preserve.
15. 'Concys' means quinces, which the egg yolks were thought to resemble. 'Chicken in Mose' (UC, 20 and RD12, 83) is the same dish, although the different name is impossible to explain.

Chicken in Gravy

Take chickens and roast them, then chop them small and fry them; then take wine or pepper[16] or vinegar and grind it together with these chickens. Mix it well with egg yolks and colour it with saffron and serve it forth. (LCC, 49)

Chicken in Musy

Take small chickens and make them clean and chop them, and put them in a pot, and add good broth of fresh meat and wine, and let them boil. And add to this sage and parsley, cut small, and ground pepper and whole cloves and maces and pine nuts and currants, and colour it up with saffron. And take raw egg yolks and draw them into the pot through a strainer, and let it all cook together, and when you take it off add a little verjuice and serve it forth. (Ar 334, 56)

Corat

Take the offal of calf, swine, or sheep; parboil them and dice them. Put them into good broth and add herbs and green spring onions cut small; cook it until tender and stir in yolks of eggs. Add verjuice, saffron, mild spice powder and salt, and serve it forth. (FC, 14)

Cretyne

Take chickens and scald them, and boil them; and grind ginger or pepper and cumin, and mix it with good milk, and put in the chickens and boil them, and serve it forth.[17] (DS, 24)

Cullis

Take chickens and scald them well, and boil them afterwards; and take the flesh and chop it small, and grind it with oats in a mortar along with white

---

16. *Sic;* there is no other recipe to check this against. There is one with the same title, but it simply tells us to treat chicken the same way as the rabbits in the preceding recipe, which is nothing like this one.

17. Later versions tend to be much more elaborate, usually calling for the addition of boiled eggs at some point.

bread, and mix it with the broth. Take the large bones and grind them all to dust and put them in the broth, and strain it through a cloth, and boil it and serve it forth.[18] (DS, 11)

Curlews *see* **Pheasants**

Dage ('Jagged' pork) [19]

Take ground boiled pork and drained rice and put it in a pot with the broth of the same pork, with sanders, spice powder, and sugar. Season it with vinegar. When it is served, put on it almonds fried and cut up, minced ginger, and ground ginger. (OP, 73)

Diacre [20]

[Chickens] shall be well boiled in fresh water until they are done, then take them and chop them into small pieces; and when they are done, mix a good almond milk with the broth and with wine, and mix it with amydon or rice flour. Then take fresh grease and put alkenet in it, and take up the colour of it; and lay the quarters [21] 5 or 6 in a dish, however it turns out, and salt it at the dresser. Sprinkle it [with the alkenet dye] with a feather or two here and there about the dish; and if you want to put ground ginger in it, not on top but in the pottage, and then serve it forth. (H279 PD, 137)

Diverse Desire [22]

Grind raisins; draw them up with osay or with sweet wine so that it is somewhat thin. Put it in a pot; mince dates and add them, and currants,

---

18. Later versions may omit the ground bones and add seasonings. A fish-day adaptation calls for fish and almond milk
19. Apparently named for the garnish.
20. In H279, 'Chicken in dropeye', incorrectly lemmatized as 'Droppe' in the *Concordance*, but this is clearly a later version of 'Diacre' in AN B, 22 and DC, 22; both names indicate the way it is decorated.
21. This contradicts the directions above to chop the chickens into small pieces, but that is probably correct, considering that this is a pottage.
22. No relation to Blancdesire; part of it however, is apparently represented (rather more clearly) by Douce Desire (page 176, below). The present recipe is a series of spiced dishes, some of which are pottages, others in other categories – but it is all one interconnected recipe.

cloves, maces, ground pepper, and Lombard powder[23] and sugar. Take pigs scalded clean, or kid or lamb or rabbit or chickens, chopped into small pieces, and fry them, and add to the sauce. Boil it and season it with ground ginger and salt. And if you wish take vinegar and make it somewhat sour, and serve it forth.

And if you wish, grind almonds and make in the same way, and colour with turnesole, or let it be white – as you wish. And if you wish you can make a pastry of eggs and sifted flour, and make it into a thin leaf, and boil it in small pellets or else in pills, and fry them in white grease. Take out the flesh; and when the sauce boils, add it[24] to it and serve. Or, if you wish, make leaves of pastry and wrap in them flesh of capons and pork, boiled and ground, and season with ground spices and salt. Make pellets of them, each pellet as big as a finger; see that it is well closed up and fried. Put it in dishes and pour the sauce over, and don't put any vinegar in it.

If you want to have a very thick pottage of it, make it thicker and serve it like the mortrews you make of raisins, and of the same colour as what you made before, and divide with the other in dishes. And if you want to make a baked dish of it, you can put each of them by themselves, or you can divide them together, and serve forth as you wish, hot or cold, and strew on a garnish of minced ginger and anise in comfit and white powder[25] and serve it forth whether it be in form of pottage or of baked food, whichever you wish.

You can dilute it with egg yolks, if you wish, after boiling it: take some of the same wine and set it on the fire in a pot, and when it boils have egg yolks drawn through a strainer into a bowl, and pour in the wine softly and gently, stirring it firmly in the bowl so it will not curdle, and see that it is very thick with yolks, and add it to that other sauce you made before. Stir it well together; serve it forth; see that there is no vinegar in it. See that it is sweet and somewhat sharp from the spice powders.

And if you wish to make it of fish, you can do it the same way you did with the flesh. Take fresh salmon, bass, and mullet, split and chopped in pieces and fried; and treat this as you did the flesh. Or take a perch, or else

23. A mixed spice powder.
24. The pellets?
25. See recipe in Chapter 1, page 22, above.

a haddock or bass, boiled; pick out the bones. Grind it and mix it with good ground spices and salt, and make it into round pellets. Then have a batter of almond milk and put the pellets in it. Take them up and fry them in oil; roll them around. Lay them in dishes and pour the sauce over, and if you wish you can treat flesh in the same way. (OP, 97)

Douce Jame

Take good cow's milk and put it in a pot. Take parsley, sage, hyssop, savory, and other good herbs; chop them and put them in the milk and boil them. Take capons half roasted and chop them in pieces [and put them in the sauce], and add pine nuts and clarified honey; salt it and colour it with saffron, and serve it forth. (FC, 64)

Douce Saracen

Chop small chickens into gobbets; wash them and put them in a pot with grease, saffron, and ground clean cinnamon. Fry them well. Wash large raisins with wine or ale; grind them small and mix them with good wine; strain them. Take this liquid and add it to the chickens when they have been fried; add cloves, mace, cubebs, ground cinnamon, and thicken it with amydon. Colour it brown according to the sauce; serve it forth.[26] (RD12, 174)

French Poach [27]

Take figs and raisins; wash them and grind them small. Draw them through a strainer with almond milk, and mix in amydon and white bread mixed with the same milk. Add dates and prunes of damson plums, then cut up pine nuts and fry them. Take chicken meat and grind it, and mix this together. Then take pepper, saffron, sanders, ground cinnamon, cloves, vinegar, sugar, and salt, and let it boil, then serve it forth. (P, 102)

Magpies *see* **Peony Pottage**

26. Somewhat contradictory: English 'Saracen' dishes were usually red, not brown. See the second paragraph of 'Pellets in Saracen Sauce' below.
27. A title which makes no apparent sense.

.

Maundemene (Pork in a sweet spiced sauce)

Take figs and raisins and boil them in wine, then grind them in a mortar and draw them through a strainer. Take fresh pork and chop it. Mix it with almond milk drawn with fresh broth, then put it all in a pot together and add cloves, cinnamon, pepper, with a little ground ginger, vinegar, sanders, and sugar. Then bake it gently and spread it on dishes. On top put pared ginger with anise in comfit, and then serve it forth. (P, 99)

Mawmene

Wine; capon meat, ground thoroughly and boiled with the wine; dry-ground almonds added; add ground cloves together with fried almonds, and there should be beef, pork, or mutton, ground; sugar to balance the strength of the spices; the colour, red or indigo.[28] (AN B, 7)

Mortrews (Pottage ground in a mortar)

Take chickens and pork and boil them together. Take the meat of the chickens and the pork and chop it small, and grind it all to dust, along with white bread; and mix it with the same broth and with eggs. Colour it with saffron and boil it, and put it in dishes, and put on them ground pepper and ginger, and serve it forth.[29] (DS, 5)

Mounchelate (Veal or mutton stew)

Take veal or mutton and chop it into gobbets. Boil it in good broth; add a good quantity of chopped herbs and a quantity of minced onions, strong spice powder, and saffron; mix in eggs and verjuice: but do not let it boil afterwards. (FC, 18)

28. This popular dish had many variations. 'Mawmene Royal' adds pine nuts, almonds, and sugar, among other things, and 'Mawmene Furnez' directs us to put the mawmene in small pastry cases and bake it. 'Mawmene Bastard' contained pine nuts and currants, but no poultry or other meat.
29. 'Mortrews in Lent' uses only the fish broth in place of eggs, but most 'Mortrews of Fish' (including 'Mortrews of Whelks', CCC, 88) call for almond milk, and 'White Mortrews' (of pork) substitutes rice flour. 'Mortrews Eweas' calls for ground boiled capon or pheasant, with wine and bread, and 'Mortrews of Lungs' is made of fish lungs and livers.

Mutton Broth

Take mutton and cut it in pieces; boil it in a pot. Add a thickening of bread, pepper, saffron, and minced onions with parsley, and serve it forth. (P, 219)

Mutton, Tripe of

Take the stomach of a sheep and make it clean, and put it in a pot of boiling water, and skim it clean, and gather the grease away, and boil it until it is tender. Then lay it on a clean board and cut it into small pieces the width of a penny, and put it in an earthen pot with strong broth of beef or mutton. Then take parsley leaves and cut them up and add them, and let it all boil together until it is tender; then take ground ginger and verjuice and saffron and salt, add them, and let it boil together, and serve it in. (H279 PD, 9)

Noumbles (Offal)

Take the offal of the venison and wash them clean in water, and salt them, and boil them in two waters. Grind pepper, bread, and ale, and mix it with the second broth and boil it; and chop the offal and put that in, and serve it forth.[30] (DS, 12)

Nut Pottage (Pottage with hazel leaves and nuts)

Take a large portion of hazel leaves and grind in a mortar as finely as you can while they are young; then draw up milk of blanched almonds mixed with fresh broth. Wring out all the juice of the leaves. Take meat of pork or capon and grind it finely; mix it with the milk and put it in a pot, with the juice of the leaves, and put it over the fire and let it boil. Take rice flour and mix it in, then add enough sugar, a quantity of vinegar, and ground ginger, saffron, and salt. Take small nuts; break them and take out the kernels and make them white [i.e., peel the inner skin] and fry them in grease; place them on your food and serve forth. (H279 PD, 141)

---

30. Other recipes are apt to use wine and some add onions; 'Noumbles of Porpoise' are made the same way, and 'Noumbles in Lent' substitutes fish stomachs and blood for the offal.

Olyotes (A thick, spicy mixed pottage)

Take good sugar and wine and blend them; add good ground ginger, galingale, and cinnamon. Take parsley juice and rice flour and meat of capons, and grind together; add to the wine mixture with sanders and saffron. Mix it with yolks of eggs; make it thick and arrange it for serving. On top, put mace, cubebs, and cloves. (RD12, 180)

Partridge, Stewed

Take good marrow and broth of beef or mutton, and when it is well cooked take the broth out of the pot and strain it through a strainer and put it in an earthen pot. Then take a good quantity of wine, about half as much, and add it; then take the partridge and stuff it with whole pepper and marrow, then sew the vents of the partridge and take cloves and maces and whole pepper and put it in the pot, and let it all boil together. And when the partridge is boiled enough, take the pot from the fire, and when you want to serve it add to the pot ground ginger, salt, and saffron, and serve it forth. (H279 PD, 18)

Partridges *see also* Pheasants; Peony Pottage

Pheasants, Partridges, Capons and Curlews, Boiled

Take good broth and put the fowl in it, and add whole pepper and ground cinnamon, a good quantity, and let them boil together; and serve it forth with mild spice powder. (FC, 37)

Pellets in Saracen Sauce

Take fresh pork or mutton, boiled; pick out the bones, cut up the meat in small pieces and grind it fine in a mortar, and mix it with eggs in the grinding. Add to it pepper, saffron, and salt. Take fresh broth, strained clean; set it on the fire in a large container. Let it boil, then season it with the same colour [yellow with saffron?]. Then make small, round balls: put them in the boiling broth and let them boil there until they are done. Then take them up and let them dry, and let your broth cool. Blow off the fat.

Take almonds; wash them and mix them with the same broth, drawing up a sort of almond milk. Put the milk in a clean pot and set it on the fire, adding to it ground pepper and cinnamon and some sanders to colour it

Saracen colour: see that most of the colour is of its own kind. Put in cloves, maces, currants, and let it boil as seems good to you. If it is too thick, thin it with sweet wine and add sugar. When your spices are tender, put the pellets into this broth. Give them a taste of ground pepper, of ginger, and verjuice, and serve the pellets in the broth, three or four in a dish, as a pottage for the second course. (OP, 17)

Peony Pottage (Pottage decorated with peonies)

Take partridges and magpies and roast them until they are half done; then take broth of chicken and of fresh boiled beef, and take bread and steep it in this broth and draw it through a strainer, and take ground ginger and grain of Paris and pepper, the same amount of each; and mix them together. And quarter your partridges and magpies and put them in a pot, and add all these things to them and boil them together, and salt it; and decorate the tops of the dishes with peony flowers and seeds, and serve forth in a mannerly way. (UC, 2)

Pig's Feet in Egredouce

Boil pigs' feet, pork, or chickens; when they are parboiled, take them up and take off the skin. Chop parsley and onions small; add this to the pigs' feet, pork or chickens along with currants and minced dates. Take vinegar, and add galantine to it. Add to this ground pepper and cinnamon, salt, saffron, and honey. Arrange your meat in dishes; pour this sauce over, and give forth. (CCC, 72)

Pigeons, Stewed

Take pigeons and stuff them with peeled garlic and with good herbs, chopped, and put them in an earthen pot; add good broth and white grease, strong spice powder, saffron, verjuice, and salt. (FC, 49)

Pork, Carvel of (Pottage of pork brains)

Take pork brains; parboil them and grind it finely, and mix it with yolks of eggs. Set it over the fire with white grease, and do not let it cook too quickly. Add to it saffron and strong spice powder, and arrange it for serving; add mild spice powder and serve it forth. (FC, 34)

Pork, Legs of, in Sauce

Take a leg or legs of pork and boil them tender, then take a great portion of onions, minced finely, with rosemary and thyme, and boil them tender in the broth; add to this cloves, maces, pepper, sanders, and salt, and serve it forth. (P, 203)

Pork, White Mortrews of (Pork pudding with almonds)

Take lean pork and boil it; blanch almonds and grind them, and mix them with the broth of the pork, and stir in rice flour, and let it all boil together, but see that the pork is ground finely enough. Add minced almonds fried in fresh grease, then arrange them all up flat in a dish; give it enough sugar and salt, and at the dresser, strew on it ground ginger mixed with almonds. (H279 PD, 120)

Rabbit in Civy

Take rabbits and chop them in pieces and cook them in good broth; mince onions and cook them in grease and good broth, and add this. Draw up a thickening of bread, blood, vinegar, and broth; put it in with strong spice powder.[31] (FC, 27)

Rabbit in Clear Broth

Take rabbits and chop them into gobbets, and wash them, and put them in fresh water and wine; boil them and skim them. And when they are boiled, pick them clean and draw the broth through a strainer, and put the meat with it in a pot and stew it, and add vinegar and ground ginger, a great quantity, and salt after the last boiling, and serve it forth. (FC, 67)

Rabbit in Egredouce (Rabbit in sweet and sour sauce)

Take parboiled rabbits and chop them, and take clean-washed dates and currants ground in a mortar, and draw them up with wine, and put all this in a pot, adding cloves, maces, pine nuts, and sugar, saffron, and strained cinnamon. In taking it off the fire, add vinegar so that it will be somewhat sharp and ground pepper and ginger; and serve it forth. (Ar 334, 148)

31. 'Rabbits in Hodgepodge' (H5401, 52) sounds like another civy: the rabbits are to be cooked in their own grease plus ale or wine and minced onions.

Spanish Dish (Minced chicken with pistachios)

Almond milk, rice flour, chicken meat; a measure of ground pistachio nuts put on top, seasoned with ground cloves to enhance the aroma of the pistachio nuts; the colour, yellow. (AN B, 4)

Sturmye (Pork in an almond milk sauce)

Take good milk of almonds drawn with wine. Take pork and chop it small; put it in a mortar and grind it fine, then put it in the same milk and put it in a pot. Take sanders and rice flour; mix them with the milk and draw them through a strainer, and put it in a clean pot: look that it be thick enough. Take sugar and honey, and put them in it; put it over the fire and let it boil a great while. Stir it well.

Take hard-boiled eggs and take the whites and cut them up as small as you can, and put them in the pot. Take saffron and add that, with ground ginger, cinnamon, galingale, and cloves, and see that you have enough spice powder; put it in the pot and mix in vinegar. Take salt and add it, mixing them well together. Make a sauce: the first part shall be wine and the second sugar or honey; boil it, stir it, and skim it clean. Wet your dishes with this and serve it forth. (H279, 112)

A Summer Pottage (Almond-milk soup with meatballs)

Take fillets of pork and veal, ground in a mortar raw, and as you grind it mix your meat with eggs. Then put your meat in a clean bowl and mix in ground cloves and pepper, and salt, and colour it with saffron. Mix it together well, and make small balls of this. Put them on the fire in a pot of boiling water, and when they are well boiled put them in a clean bowl. Then take almond milk made with broth of fresh beef and put it in a clean pot; add cloves, mace, pine nuts, currants, and coarsely minced ginger, then set the pot on the fire and stir it together well. Put the meatballs in the pot and boil them briefly. Colour it the colour of a cawdel [i.e., yellow], salt it, and serve it forth. (NBC, 1)

Summer Soup

To make a summer soup, take almond milk and mix it with fresh broth. Then take young pork, boil it and chop it and grind it, and moisten it with the milk and put it back on the fire. Then take rice flour, almond milk, saffron, powdered ginger and cinnamon, put them through a strainer and add to the pot, and stir it well to prevent lumps, and set it on the fire and add sugar to it. And ladle out as many servings as you wish in dishes, and sprinkle them with red candied anise seeds, and serve them. (NBC, 59)

Tars Curtays (Ground chicken in an almond milk sauce)

Take figs and raisins; grind them small in a mortar and take them up and wring them through a cloth. Take cloves and sugar and add them. Take meat of chickens and grind it small, and draw it up with almond milk, and add more milk to it if you wish. Let it boil together, then take maces, cloves, and cubebs and put on top, and so serve it forth. (Sl 1108, 124)

Venison in Broth

Take parsley and hyssop and sage, and chop it small. Boil it [herbs and meat] in wine and water and a little ground pepper, and serve it forth. (DS, 54)

Venison in Sauce

Take the meat of a deer and pick it clean and parboil it, then take it up and dry it with a cloth, and chop it into gobbets, and put it in a pot. Add wine and let it boil. Take sage, parsley, hyssop, and chop it small, and add ground pepper and cloves and cinnamon, and colour it with blood, and let it boil, and serve it forth. (Ar 334, 18)

Fish-based

Ballock Broth

Take eels and flay them and carve them into pieces, and put them to boil in water and wine so that they are well covered. Add to this sage and other herbs, with a few minced onions. When the eels are cooked enough, put them in a container; take a pike and cut it into gobbets and boil it in the same broth. Add to this ground ginger, galingale, cinnamon, and pepper; salt it and put the eels in it, and serve it forth. (FC, 112)

Chauden for Lent

Take blood of gurnards and conger, and the stomachs of gurnards and boil them tender and mince them small, and make a thickening of white crusts and minced onions. Grind it all in a mortar, and then boil it together until it is very thick; then take vinegar [wine or cider] and saffron and add it, and serve it forth. (FC, 118)

Cockles *see* Mussels

Cockles of Cod

To boil codling or cod, take a cod and cut it in small pieces and put it in broth of fresh salmon and boil it. Add almond milk and soaked bread, and colour it with sanders and saffron; add sugar and ground pepper, and serve it with other fish, such as turbot, pike and salmon, chopped; season it with vinegar and salt and serve it. (NBC, 180)

Dogfish, Stewed

Take speckled red dogfish; flay off the skin. Draw it, chop it in pieces. Put it in a pot. Chop the liver small and add it [with] broth of fresh fish. Take ground pepper and minced onions; add them. Boil it up. Season it with ground ginger and verjuice; colour it with saffron, galantine,[32] and salt. (RD12, 22)

Eel in Brasee

Take eels and boil them whole, and slip the flesh from the bone and beat it in a mortar with parboiled dates, and dilute it with almond milk and put it in the pot; add to this sugar, ground pepper, and cloves. Then colour it with saffron and sanders, and make your pottage very thick; arrange it in dishes in slices, and sprinkle with ground ginger mixed with sugar and sanders, and serve it.[33] (NBC, 42)

Eel in Gravy

Take almonds and grind them, and mix them with sweet wine, and put it in a pot; and add whole slices of eels and cloves and maces and currants

32.   See the recipe for this standard sauce in Chapter 10, page 148, below.
33.   Two almost identical recipes appear in Ar 334, but the second is elaborated: adding, for example, cod livers.

and pine nuts and minced ginger, and let it boil; colour it with sanders, and on taking it off add a little vinegar mixed with ground cinnamon, and serve forth. (Ar 334, 105)

Herring, Stewed

See that your herrings are well watered and take out the bone, and take the roe and lay them in a dish of water, and wash both the herring and the roe together. Then take a little parsley and as much thyme and a few onions, and mix all together as finely as you can; then crush all the herbs and the roe together, and take a little ground pepper and sugar and currants and a little ground white bread, and put all these together and stuff your herrings with them. When they are stuffed, lay them on a dish, and take a good portion of ale, and add mustard to it, and put great raisins over them, and cover them with a dish and set them on the fire; and thus serve them forth. (P1047, 33)

Mussels

Boil mussels and them chop them roughly and mix them with almond milk and make a thick pottage; colour it with saffron. You may do the same with cockles or periwinkles.[34] (H5402 1)

Mussels in Broth

Take mussels and pick them over; boil them in their own broth. Make a thickener of crusts of bread and vinegar; add to it minced onions, and add the mussels to this and boil it. Put in strong spice powder with a little salt and saffron; and cook oysters the same way.[35] (FC, 125)

Mussels in the Shell

Take and pick over good mussels and put them in a pot; add to them minced onions and a good quantity of pepper and wine, and a little vinegar. As soon as they begin to gape, take them from the fire, and serve hot in a dish with the same broth. (H4016, 106)

34. To a similar pottage of ground mussels, DC, 63 adds chestnuts, oddly.
35. Some recipes call for only broth, or wine rather than vinegar, as do 'Mussels in Gravy' (H5401, 87) and 'Mussels in Sauce' (Ar 334, 100) which are otherwise identical.

Mussels, Caudle of

Take mussels and boil them; pick them clean and wash them clean in wine. Take almonds and grind them. Take some of the mussels and grind them, and chop some small; mix the ground mussels with their broth. Mix the almonds with clear water. Put all these together and add verjuice and vinegar. Take white of leeks and parboil them well; wring out the water and chop them small. Add oil to them [all this?], with onions parboiled and finely minced; add to this strong spice powder, saffron, and a little salt. Boil it, but do not make it too thick, and serve it forth. (FC, 127)

Mussels, Porre of (Ground leeks and mussels)

Take mussel broth, and grind your leeks in a mortar with a little oatmeal, and boil them well; grind your mussels and add them, and boil it all together. (LCC, 109)

Oyster Pottage

Parboil your oysters and take them out, keeping the broth; chop them finely on a board and grind them in a mortar. Put them in their own broth along with almond milk, and mix in amydon; fry finely minced onions in oil, or boil them in milk, and add [them, with] ground spices. Colour it with saffron. (LCC, 31)

Oysters in Civy (Oysters in onion sauce)

Take oysters; parboil them in their own broth. Make a thickening of crusts of bread and mix it with the broth, with vinegar. Mince onions and add to this, with herbs, and add the oysters. Boil it, and add strong spice powder and salt; serve it forth. (FC, 126)

Oysters in Gravy (A thick oyster stew)

Shell oysters and boil them in wine and their own broth; strain the broth through a cloth. Take blanched almonds; grind them and mix them with the same broth, and add rice flour, and put the oysters in it. Add ground ginger, sugar, maces, cubebs, and salt; boil it, but do not make it too thick, and serve it forth.[36] (FC, 124)

---

36. 'Oysters in Gravy, Bastard' calls for ale and bread instead of almond milk and rice flour.

Oysters *see also* Mussels in Broth

Periwinkles *see* Mussels

Pike in Latimer sauce

Split pikes; chop them in pieces. Put them in a pot with water, red wine, and the contents of the stomachs of more pikes, cut small, if you have them. Set it on the fire, and when it has boiled enough season it with ground ginger, verjuice, and salt. Cut white bread into small sops and put them in dishes, with the sauce on top.[37] (RD12, 38)

Pike, Boiled

Take and make sauce of water, salt, and a little ale and parsley, and then take a pike and nape it and draw it in the belly, and slit it into pieces through the belly, back, head, and tail with a knife. And cut the sides into quarters, and wash it clean; and if you want to have it round, slit it in the head, in the back, and draw it there, and slit it in two or three places in the back, but not through. And slit the stomach, and keep the liver, and cut away the gall. And when the sauce begins to boil, skim it, and wash the pike and put it in it, and put in the stomach and the liver too, and let them boil together. Then make the sauce thus: mince the stomach and the liver in a little of the fat of the pike, and add to it ground ginger, verjuice, mustard, and salt, and serve it forth all hot. (H4016, 150)

Porpoise in Galantine

Take porpoise: discard the skin. Cut it in small slices no larger than a finger, or less. Take bread mixed with red wine and add ground cinnamon and pepper. Boil it; season it up with ground ginger, vinegar, and salt. (OP, 27)

Porpoise, Fresh

Fresh porpoise shall be chopped into gobbets with the blood. Then grind ginger and pepper and bread with wine and ale; boil it, & &c. (W1, 147)

---

37.   The version of this dish in CCC is somewhat more elaborate.

Porpoise, Noumbles of

Parboil the offal of porpoise, and if you wish some of the fish; cut it small and put it in a pot. Draw up a thickener of crusts of bread with the same broth and some of the blood, and red wine. Put it together in a pot with ground pepper, cloves, and cinnamon; boil it, stir it, and season it up with ground ginger, vinegar, and salt. Make offal of venison in the same way, and of codling, of conger, and of other good fish also, and serve them forth. (OP, 26)

Pudding in Lent or on Fish Days

Take the stomach of a pike, cod, or fresh ling, or a nice small pocket of linen cloth, or else the back of the cod or the ling with what cleaves to it. Chop all these [the contents, not the stomach itself] small to make your pudding minced. For the stuffing, take the liver of the cod or ling and a piece of the same fish, or a piece of fresh salmon, and chop it finely, and draw it up with the broth of their fishes through a strainer. Add currants, salt, and saffron, and fill the stomach reasonably. Simmer it over a slow fire, then boil it and serve it forth. (CUL, 181)

Salmon, Caudle of

Take the guts of salmon and make them clean; parboil them a little. Take them up and dice them. Slit the white of leeks and carve them into small pieces; strain the broth and put the leeks in it with oil, and let it all boil together. Put in the cut-up salmon. Make a thickener of almond milk and bread, and add spices, saffron, and salt; boil it well and see that it is not too thick. (FC, 114)

Turbot or Codling

Take the stomachs of turbot, haddock, or codling and pick them clean and scrape them and wash them clean, and parboil them in good fresh broth of turbot or salmon or pike; then cut parsley small and add it, and cut the stomachs to a penny's width, and put all together in a pot and let it boil together. When they are boiled tender, add saffron and salt and verjuice and ground ginger, and serve forth. (H279 PD, 60)

Whelk Pottage

Take whelks and scour them well with water and salt, and then chop them on a board as small as you can, and then grind them well in a mortar. Then boil them in milk of almonds or cow's milk, and mix it with amydon, and colour it with saffron, and put in it cumin or pepper or other ground spices. (DC, 61)

Whelks, Mortrews of

Boil your whelks tender with water and salt, then take them out of the shell. Pick out the guts and the hat, then wash them in two waters or three. Then boil water with sugar and salt and with it make milk of blanched almonds. Put it in a pot; make it scalding hot. Then chop your whelks on a clean board, and while chopping sprinkle over some of this milk, or else they will slide away. Then grind them and put them in the pot with the milk. Add to this grated wastel bread and make it very thick. Colour with saffron, salt it. And a hundred whelks, or half a hundred, with one pound of almonds is enough for eight dishes. Put over the dish a garnish of sugar and ground ginger, and give forth. (CCC, 88)

CHAPTER FIVE

Special Types of Pottages

The special types of pottages listed here begin with 'Brewets', often translated 'Broths', which were usually unthickened – or, if thickened at all, lightly so: the recipes sometimes warn us that the mixture should be thin. 'Sliced Food' represents the opposite case: pottages cooked until their sauces were thick enough to be served in slices. 'Gruels and Sops' were often food for invalids, particularly the 'Gruels', but both were sometimes served to normal diners also. A composite of 'Four Recipes for Invalids' is given at the beginning of this section to indicate its utility, including, as it does, both types.

The fourth group, 'Jellied Dishes', often turns up among the last dishes of a course or menu, suggesting that they were regarded as festive: but in fact, they were as much practical expedients as decorative special dishes, since fish or meat preserved in its own jelly evidently kept longer in the pantry. Finally, we have a few pasta recipes, perhaps surprisingly for England at this early date.

Brewets

Brewet Diverse

Take rabbits, small kids, veal, or young pigs; chop them in pieces. When it has been parboiled, put it in a pot and add to it fresh broth and wine. Fry together onions minced finely, currants, minced dates, and pine nuts, then put them in the brewet and let it boil. Add ground cinnamon, maces, cubebs, sanders, saffron, sugar, vinegar, and salt.

See that it has a sharp edge. Mix in almond milk and amydon, and then serve it forth. (P, 109)

Brewet of Chicken

Chicken in brewet shall be scalded and boiled with pork; and grind pepper and cumin, bread and ale, and mix this with the broth and boil it, and colour it with saffron and salt it, and serve it forth.[1] (DS, 7)

Brewet of Hare

Take and chop your hare into pieces and boil it in good broth and its own blood. When it is cooked, draw [the broth] through a strainer. Then take almond milk and mix it with this broth; add parboiled onions, cut small, to the pot, and add vinegar and salt and serve it. (NBC, 247)

Brewet of Kid

Take a kid or veal, chopped, parboiled, and drained; put it in a pot. Take almonds and add them, drawn up with fresh broth. Add whole cloves and mix it with rice flour, and put in grease; and after boiling it, season it up with vinegar, ground pepper, ginger, and cinnamon and sugar and salt, and serve it forth. (OP, 54)

Brewet Mose

Take parsley, hyssop, savory, clarry, violet, and avens; grind them all together and push it through a strainer. Then take good pork and chicken meat and grind it small; mix it with fresh broth and the juice of the herbs. Then set it on the fire and let it boil, and add to it cloves, cinnamon, ginger, pepper, saffron, vinegar, sugar, yolks of eggs, and salt. Give it a little more heat and then serve it forth. (P, 110)

Brewet Salmene

Vinegar, galingale, cinnamon, ground cloves, a great deal of many eggs, and plenty of sugar to balance the strength of the spicing. Mix ginger with the spices; the colour should be black or green.[2] (DC, 17)

---

1. Some recipes call for wine rather than ale and/or call for different seasonings.
2. A later recipe (H279 PD, 80) calls for fish instead of eggs, as do contemporary French recipes.

Brewet Saracen

Take almonds and grind them, and mix them with beef broth, and make a good thick milk, and put it in a pot; and add cloves, maces, pine nuts, currants, and minced ginger, and let it boil. And take bread and steep it in sweet wine and draw it up, and add it to the pot with sugar. Then take rabbits and parboil them, or squirrels, and fry them, and parboiled partridges: also fry them whole for a lord, or else chop them in gobbets, and when they are almost fried add them to the pot and let them all boil together.

Colour it with sanders and saffron, and add vinegar and ground cinnamon strained with wine, and give it a boil; then take it from the fire, and see that your pottage is thin, and add to it a good deal of ground ginger. Serve it forth, a whole rabbit or a squirrel or a partridge, for a lord. (Ar 334, 52)

Brewet Sec

Fresh broth, grapes' verjuice, ground parsley added; cloves, maces, cubebs; in the season for chickens, after Easter. It should have a good savour of spices, with saffron boiled with the parsley in the broth; the colour, yellow.[3] (DC, 16)

Brewet without Herbs

To make brewet without herbs, bread, saffron, or eggs, take pork, hens, and goose giblets and boil together; then take the grease of a goose, kid, roebuck, or hog, and cook [the meat] in good rich broth [i.e., enriched with the grease]; grind the meat; take fine grease, pour it on top, and then serve. (AN A, 10)

Cinnamon Brewet

Take chickens and boil them in water, then grind blanched almonds and dilute them, half with the broth of the chickens and half with pure water. Take a great deal of cinnamon and a little ginger and grind this with your [almond] milk. Add sugar to it. Boil all this together; stir it well while it

---

3.   Two later recipes call for wine rather than verjuice, and add dates, but verjuice is no doubt correct, to give the 'sharp' (sec) flavour, and dates, which are sweet, are clearly inappropiate here.

is on the fire. Add to it a little white grease when you put your sugar in. Then take your chickens and chop them in pieces and put them in the brewet. If you wish, you may put in meat of capons or hens, pheasants or partridges. And beware when you take it from the fire: do not put it on the cold ground, for if you do the food will lose its savour. (RD12, 185)

Cold Brewet

Take cream of almonds; dry it in a cloth and when it is dried put it in a container. Add to it salt, sugar, and ground ginger, and the juice of fennel, and wine, and let it stand well by the fennel, and dress it, and serve it forth.[4] (FC, 135)

Eel in Brewet

Eels shall be flayed and cut in gobbets and boiled; and grind pepper, and saffron or mint and parsley, and bread and ale, and mix it with the broth, and boil it and serve it forth.[5] (DS, 74)

Eggs in Brewet

Take water and butter and boil them together with saffron and gobbets of cheese. Wring eggs through a strainer, and when the water has boiled for a while take the eggs and beat them with verjuice and add them to the water; set it over the fire, and do not let it boil, and serve it forth.[6] (FC, 93)

German Brewet

Take almonds and draw a good milk from them with water; take capons, rabbits, or partridges and chop the capon, or kid, or chickens or rabbits: partridge should be left whole. Then blanch the meat and put it in the milk; take lard and mince it, and add that. Take onions and mince them,

---

4. Another FC recipe adds meat and more spices, and one in Ar 334 calls for fried chicken and omits fennel entirely; but one in H5401 duplicates this one almost exactly.
5. Most other recipes add onions to this brewet; one such (H279 PD, 89) is mistitled 'Eel in Gauncele': a 'gauncele' should contain garlic, which is not called for here.
6. Other recipes for this add fresh milk, and put in the eggs, unbeaten, earlier and the cheese later.

and add enough of them, and cloves and small raisins as well. Put in whole saffron and put it to the fire, and stir it well; when the meat is done, take it off and add enough sugar. Take ground ginger, galingale, and cinnamon, and mix the powder with vinegar; put this in the brewet, season it with salt, and serve forth.[7] (H279 PD, 67)

German Brewet in Lent

Take fine thick milk of almonds; take dates, and mince them finely into it. Take enough sugar and strew on it, and a little rice flour. Serve it forth white, and see that it is not too thick. (H279 PD, 68)

White German Brewet

Take kids or chickens and cut them into morsels, and boil them in almond milk or cow's milk. Grind ginger and galingale and put that in it, and boil it and serve it forth.[8] (DS, 13)

Lamprey in Brewet

Take lamprays and scald them, then roast them on a gridiron; and grind pepper and saffron, mix it with ale and put the lamprays in this. (P1047, 21)

Lombard Brewet

Take hens, chickens, rabbits, or other meat, boiled; put it in a pot. Add almond milk and pepper, and mix it with bread, and put in hard-boiled yolks of eggs ground and blended with parsley; add a little grease or clarified butter or pork fat, and season it with spice powder, salt, and vinegar, and make it as red as blood. (OP, 45)

---

7. Probably the directions should have called for frying the onions in the lard, not just putting in both as ingredients. The distinctive characteristic of the dish seems to have originally been a combination of almond milk and fried onions, but this got confused in English versions, which often dropped the onions completely, as in the variants noted below. Two recipes which call for 'small birds' in a sauce of almond milk and fried onions and thus ought to be entitled 'German Brewet' are called, oddly, 'Drepe', FC, 21, and 'Drore', Ar 334, 22; another in this group is 'Chickens in Dropeye', H279 PD, 137, which omits onions and is dyed red with alkenet.
8. Another version calls for adding grapes.

Oysters in Brewet

They shall be shelled and boiled in clean water. Grind pepper, saffron, bread, and ale, and mix it with broth. Put in your oysters and boil it and salt it and serve it forth. (DS, 73)

Pike in Brewet

Take the pike and scale it; wash it clean and cut it in pieces, and put it in a pot with good wine; and when it is in the pot, add half a pound of cinnamon and another of currants, and a handful of parsley, and a good quantity of sugar, and boil it all together until it is thick enough. Colour it with saffron, and when it is done add a good portion of ginger, and then take up the pike and arrange it in dishes, and cut sops not as long as a brewis, and lay them in the dishes with the pike, and pour the sauce over it and serve it forth.[9] (TCCo, 92)

Rabbit, Cold Brewet of

Grind raisins or dates; draw them up with osey. Add to this cream of almonds and a great deal of ground cinnamon, drawn with sweet wine; Lombard powder,[10] ground grains of paradise and ginger, and a little vinegar and white sugar. Set it on the fire, and when it boils take it off and put it in a bowl. Have rabbits boiled in good broth and salt; take them up and remove the meat from the bones on both sides of the back. Lay them in the sauce. Serve them forth: lay them in dishes and pour the sauce over them. Serve it forth, and if you wish you may chop them in pieces.

And if you have chickens, raise their wings and thighs, keeping them, and chop the body; when it is in the sauce, serve it forth in the same manner as a Royal Sauce.[11] (OP, 96)

---

9.   'Pike in Brewis' (RD12, 39) is a slighty more elaborate version, calling for a fish broth rather than wine and arranging the fish on toasted 'brewis' sops. 'Pike in Sauce' (OP, 62) is more complex, calling for cooking the stomach and the liver separately and mixing them with ginger sauce. See also 'Pike on Sops' below, under 'Pottages, Gruels and Sops'.
10.   A mixed spice powder.
11.   I am not sure what dish that is.

Salt Eel in Brewet

Flay the eel and cut it into gobbets. Boil it, then take small onions and peel them and boil them with the eel. Grind bread; add pepper and saffron and mix it with ale; boil it and add it to the eel. (RD12, 168)

Saracen Brewet

Take the flesh of fresh beef and cut it in pieces, and bread, and fry it in fresh grease. Take it up and dry it, and put it in a pot with wine, sugar, and ground cloves. Boil it together until the meat has absorbed the liquid. Take almond milk and cubebs, maces and cloves, and boil them together; take the meat and add it to this, and serve it forth.[12] (DS, 55)

White Saracen Brewet

Cow's milk mixed with eggs and a great deal of select ginger; in apple season, the colour white. (DC, 18)

Spanish Brewet

Take venison and slice it into long slices; fry them in butter, and moisten them with wine. Then take sugar, almond milk, cloves, maces, and cubebs; boil them together [with the venison] and season them with spice powder and vinegar, and serve it. (NBC, 186)

Tench in Brewet

Take the tench and boil it and roast it, and grind pepper and saffron, bread and ale, and mix with the broth, and boil it; then take the roasted tench and lay it on a platter and pour the sauce over it. (H279 PD, 94)

Tuscan Brewet

Take raw pork and chop it small and grind it in a mortar; mix it with beaten eggs, but not too thin. In grinding it, add ground pepper. Then

12. Most of the parallel recipes call for various meats – rabbits, squirrels, or partridges – but agree on first frying the meats, a genuine Arab practice which seems to justify the name of the dish. Two others, however, calling for yet other meats (venison, pork and capons or hens), omit this step, probably because it was an unfamiliar practice.

take up the meat in your hands and roll it into balls the size of crabs and put them in boiling water. To harden them, take them out to cool. Take fresh broth and in it put parsley, hyssop, and savory, chopped small; mix in flour or bread and colour it with saffron, adding ground pepper and cloves. Then take your balls and add them; boil it all together, and serve it forth.[13] (LCC, 1102)

Venison Brewet

Take the meat of a roebuck; chop it, parboil it, drain it, and put it in a pot. Take the same broth, or other fresh broth; draw it through a strainer and put it on the meat, with onions and herbs and whole cloves, maces and cubebs, and boil it. If need be, add crusts, or else white bread, mixed with a little of the same broth and the same blood. Colour it with saffron. Add salt and ground pepper, and a larger quantity of cinnamon, and serve it forth. (OP, 48)

Whelks in Brewet

Take whelks and boil in ale, then pick them clean; then wash them in water and salt by themselves, and first with ale and salt, and do so while they are slimy. Then put them in vinegar and lay parsley above them, and serve in. (H279, 93)

White Brewet

Blanch almonds in cold water; grind them small. Draw them up with white wine; add to them figs minced small, and put in ground ginger, sugar, and salt.[14] (Sl 7, 14)

Sliced dishes

A Simple Sliced Dish

Take the white of [boiled] eggs and chop them small in a mortar; then take a little fat broth and bread grated small, and mix them together with

13. One recipe of the same name (Ar 334, 53) is quite different, calling for pork fillets, not meatballs, with pine nuts and currants; no herbs.
14. The recipe in OP (and NBC) calls for roasted meat and a finishing touch of alkenet, so it would not be 'white' at all.

your hand, and add to it a little clean [i.e., clarified] honey and ground cinnamon and ginger, and boil it a little, and serve it forth.[15] (eM, 67)

Barleeg

Take almond cream and mix it with rice flour and add sugar. Let it boil and stir it well, and colour it with saffron and sanders, and make it very thick, and put it in dishes in slices, and serve it forth. (Ar 334, 176)

Blancdesire Mailed

Make good almond milk with water boiled with sugar and salt, and afterward second milk [see note to Almond Milk Pottage, page 23, above]. Take half a quarter pound of rice flour, or else grated white bread, and mix it with the second milk. Put this in a pot; boil it, stir it. Then set it off the fire. Take two spoonfuls of oil lukewarm on the fire, and put alkenet in it. Draw this through a strainer and into a spice dish. Then arrange the thickened almond milk in dishes, flat or sliced; sprinkle on it this alkenet solution with a few feathers, and therefore it is called 'mailed'. Alkenet may be melted with butter or with oil or with grease, and no other way.[16] (CCC, 38)

Better Brawn

Take calves' feet and scald them and boil them in wine and fresh broth until they are tender. Then take them up and lay them on a board and pick out the bones, and chop the meat and mix it with the broth, and put it in a pot with some diced sinews; then take blanched almonds, powdered pepper, a good amount of powdered cloves and a little powdered cinnamon and sanders and a little saffron. Then put it on the fire and, when it boils, add yolks of eggs, diced small, and powdered ginger, vinegar and salt, and put it in a small dish. When it is cold slice it and serve it.[17] (NBC, 63)

15. Another recipe, eM 87, omits the spices from this mixture and tells us to form it into little cakes and bake them.
16. This recipe differs from other 'Blancdesire' recipes in having no chicken or substitute for it, and in being red (with alkenet) rather than white: 'mailed' refers to this cover of red colouring. Note that again no use is suggested for the thicker 'first milk'.
17. A Lenten version of this dish is made with dried cod instead of calves' feet, and omitting the eggs, of course.

Brawn Fondue

Take sliced brawn and yolks of eggs and some of the white and flour, and strain [the batter], and add to it a good quantity of sugar and a little saffron and salt. Then heat a pan with fresh grease, and take the brawn and wet it well in the batter and put it in the pan, and when it is fried a little take it up and put your liquid on it.[18] (M 63)

Sweet and Sour Brawn

Take parboiled dates and raisins and grind them in a mortar, then draw up your mixture with vernage[19] or clarre, or else good bastard, and let this boil well. And put in it broken cloves and sugar or honey, and ground cinnamon; and in taking it off add a little vinegar mixed with ginger and cinnamon, and colour it with sanders and saffron. In the boiling, add minced ginger. Then take fresh brawn and slice it and put three slices in a dish; then take fried pine nuts, all hot, and put them in the pot, and pour the sauce around the slices and serve it forth. (H1605, 134)

White Brawn

Take fresh brawn [boar's meat or pork] and mince it fine, and take good thick milk of blanched almonds and put it all in a pot, with sugar, and let it all boil together until it is very stiff; then take it up and put it in a clean cold basin and let it stand there until it is cold. Then slice it, two or three in a dish, and serve forth.[20] (H279 LV, 2)

Chicken Neck Pudding

Take parsley, gizzard, and the liver and heart and parboil in clean water; then chop them small and put in 2 or 3 raw yolks of eggs, and chop all

18. The writer has forgotten to say what this liquid is; the title means the brawn is to be 'drowned' in whatever it is.
19. A strong, sweet wine – like the 'bastard' suggested as an alternative.
20. Recipes for 'Brawn in Comfit' follow this procedure but add a few spices and call for putting it in a linen cloth, pressing the liquid out, and serving decorated with bones. 'Royal Brawn' is basically the same, but adds directions for (optionally) dying the brawn in various colours; the most interesting of the other variants is 'Brawn Royal in Lent', made of fish and disguised as eggs, i.e. moulded in egg shells with a 'yolk' section dyed yellow.

together. Add maces and cloves and saffron and a little ground pepper, and salt, and fill [the chicken necks] up and sew them [closed], and lay them along the chicken's back, and skewer them on, and roast them, and serve forth. (H279 LV, 34)

Ferysse (Green chicken pudding)

Take hens' meat and grind it finely; then take vine leaves with the crops of the vines and parsley, and grind them finely, and draw them through a strainer with fresh broth. Then mix your meat with this liquid and put it in a good pot; add to it pepper, cloves, saffron, sugar, and salt, and mix in yolks of eggs and white amydon. Then bake it; see that it is coloured gaudy green, and serve it forth. (P, 104)

Gingerbread

Take good honey and clarify it on the fire, and take good white bread and grate it and put it in the boiling honey, and stir it well with a slice so that it will not burn to the container; and then take it off and add ginger, long pepper, and sanders, and mix it up with your hands. Put it in a flat box and strew sugar on it, and pick cloves in it around the edge and in the midst, if it please you. (GK, 19)

Haggis

Take eggs with all the white and mince bread and sheep's tallow as great as dice. Grind pepper and saffron and add them, and put this in the sheep's belly. Boil it well and serve it in broad, thin slices.[21] (DS, 15)

Leach Bastard

Take pot sugar and put it through a strainer, and grind dates as small as you can, and mix them together until they are as stiff as possible. Add ground

---

21. Some later recipes add various embellishments, such as milk or cream; one in H279 adds chopped guts, while another there adds roasted pullets, pork, cheese, and spices to the stuffing: but perhaps for good reason doesn't label this one 'haggis'. 'Fronchemoyle' (variously spelled) is another word for haggis.

pepper, cloves, sugar, and a quantity of saffron, and put it against the sun until it is stiff enough to be sliced.[22] (eM 28)

Leach Lombard (Lombard slices)

Mix together a good portion of wine and honey and set it on the fire, and when it begins to boil skim off some of the foam and set it on the fire again, and add ground pepper and cinnamon and a quantity of grated bread and stir it well together, and colour it with saffron and sanders; and when you take it off, add a little vinegar mixed with powdered ginger, and stir it together until it is stiff. Then gather it up in a cloth and let it set for a while, and leave it in the same cloth until it is cold. Then slice it and put two slices in a dish and sprinkle powdered ginger mixed with sugar on top of it, and serve it.[23] (NBC, 50)

Leach Proven (Eels in sliceable almond milk base)

Take milk of almonds; mix it with white wine and water. Take parsley and chopped onions; add eels, chopped and boil. Put in saffron, whole pepper, and whole cloves. Season it with spice powder and salt. (OP, 25)

Mange Moleyn (Capon in sliceable almond milk base)

Take almonds and blanch them, and draw them through a strainer into a pot as a thick milk; then take meat of a capon and chop it small, and put it in a pot, and mix it with rice flour. Add to this white grease[24] and boil it all together; and when it is done, take it off the fire and add enough sugar. Then take blanched almonds and fry them, and lay three slices in a dish, and on every slice prick three almonds; and then serve it forth. (H279 LV, 9)

Mawment, White (A dish based on dates)

Take a great portion of blanched almonds and grind them small and draw them up with clarrey; then add vernage to the almond mixture and draw

22. 'Leach Royal' (eM, 34) is similar but adds raisins and figs.
23. There are many variations of this dish: it may contain pork, dates, chopped almonds or currants, and/or boiled egg yolks. 'Leach Lorrey' (CUL, 113) appears to be a variant containing ground almonds and dates thickened with egg yolks or rice flour.
24. And, evidently, the almond milk.

up a running milk. Then grind a good portion of boiled dates; draw them up with the running milk, and make it thick. Then put them in a pot and boil them together until they are very thick. Then mince good dates and add them with sugar, cloves, maces, and galingale, and make of this a dragee. Arrange three or four slices [of the cooked date mixture] on a dish, and put your dragee on top, and serve it forth. (P, 223)

Lete Lardes (Roasted milk)

Take fresh milk and put it in a pan. Take eggs, with all the whites, and beat them well and add to it, and colour it with saffron, and boil it until it becomes thick; and then pass it through a strainer, and take what is left and press it on a board. And when it is cold, lard it, and cut it in slivers, and roast it on a gridiron and serve it forth.[25] (DS, 25)

Mon Ami (A cheese custard)

Take thick cream of cow's milk and boil it over the fire, then take it up and set it aside; then take sweet cow's curds and press out the whey and grind them in a mortar, and add them to that cream and boil them together. Add to this sugar and saffron and May butter; and take egg yolks, beaten and strained, and in setting down the pot beat the yolks into it, and stir it well, and make the pottage very stiff. Arrange five or seven slices in a dish, and decorate with violet flowers, and serve it forth. (Ar 334, 174)

Pear Paste Leach

Take pears and boil them, and pick them over and grind them and draw them through a strainer, and mix it with bastard; then put this in a pot with saffron and boil it with maces, cloves, ground cinnamon, cubebs, and a little ground pepper. Roll them up in your hands with bread crumbs and serve forth. (H279 LV, 16)

Sops of Salomere[26] (Pork-based slices in almond milk)

Take boiled pork and chop it and grind it; then take cow's milk and beaten eggs and saffron, and mince parsley blades and add them, and let it all boil

25. Some later recipes omit the lard which gives this its name.
26. Not a true 'sops' dish.

together, and arrange it on a cloth and carve small slices of it and put them in a dish. Then take almond milk and rice flour and sugar and saffron, and boil it all together; then pour your sauce on the slices and serve forth hot. (H279 LV, 7)

Turnesole (Pottage)

To make Tornsole, take almond milk made with vernage or with other sweet wine. Set it on the fire to boil, and add to it sugar or honey, and make it very thick with rice flour, then take it off the fire. Take blue turnesole and dip it in wine so that the wine takes the colour, and colour your pottage, and dress it up in dishes, and serve it forth, one slice blue and another white.[27] (NBC, 28)

Viande Burton

To make Viand of Bourton, take dates, figs, currants and boil them in red wine; then grind them up with pieces of bread steeped in vernage, and add that to the pot. Add cloves and cinnamon and boil it and stir it together, and as the pot boils stir in two pounds of sugar and egg yolks and a quarter of minced ginger, and when you take it off add half a quarter of ginger. Colour it with saffron and sanders and salt it, and add rose water. And, for a lord, let your pottage be thick enough to slice, and place five or six slices in a dish; and make a topping of fine sugar and ginger and candied anise, and sprinkle this on your pottage and serve it. (NBC, 48)

Viande Leach

Take cow's milk and set it over the fire, and add to it sanders, and make a stiff posset of ale [and the milk]; then hang the curds from this on a pin, in a good cloth, and let it drain. Then take it and add honey to it, and stir it together. Then fetch curds from the dairy and mix them together, and lay it in a cheese vat before it is torn into three parts or four, in linen cloth; and salt it and slice it, and serve it forth.[28] (H279 LV, 11)

---

27. Another recipe suggests using blackberries instead of turnesole.
28. This is one of more than six recipes bearing this title, but all quite different: some are meat- or fish-based, but this seems about as typical as one could find.

Viande Leach, Cold

Take quinces and pare them. Core them and cut them in small pieces, and put them in an earthen pot, and add white grease mixed with clarified honey and raw egg yolks and a little almond milk. Add powdered saffron and slice it to serve.[29] (NBC, 65)

Wastels, Stuffed (Bread, enriched, with currants)

Take a wastel [a round loaf of white bread] and hollow out the crumbs. Take eggs and sheep's tallow and the crumbs of the wastel, strong spice powder and salt, with saffron and currants: mix all these together, and put it in the wastel. Close it and bind it firmly together, and boil it well. (FC, 167)

Ynde, Pottage of (Indigo pottage)

Take almond milk made with sweet wine and put it in a pot and let it boil, and make it very thick with rice flour; add cloves and sugar and colour it with indigo suitable for pottage. Take and break it in a mortar and mix it with a little wine, and in the setting down put it in the pot and serve it forth in slices. (Ar 334, 109)

Gruels and sops

Four Recipes for Invalids

Make Ale Broth thus: with groats [oats] and saffron and good ale. Take water boiled with honey for Water Gruel made with groats. Mix white bread around in dishes and pour in boiled milk: that is called Milk Sops, to be served on Saturday nights. But don't forget Sugared Sops: toast slivers of best quality white bread and anoint them with wine on both sides; then sprinkle them with enough sugar. (LCC, 125)

Beef in Gruel

Take clear water and lean beef and let them boil; and when the beef is boiled take it up and prick it, and let it bleed into a container, and then

29. This recipe obviously omits the necessary step of cooking the quinces. Since other 'Viande Leach' dishes are also apparently served cold, it is hard to see what sets this one apart.

put the blood and the meat in a pot. Add to it oatmeal, parsley, and sage, making a good gruel of it. Draw it through a strainer and put it in a clean pot and let it boil, then add salt, and if it is not brown enough take a little blood and add it before it is completely mixed, and make it brown enough, and serve it forth.[30] (H279 PD, 24)

Alayed Sops (Sops in custard sauce)

Take milk and boil it, and then take yolks of eggs separated from the whites and draw them through a strainer; put them in the milk and set it on the fire and heat it, but do not let it boil. Stir it well until it is somewhat thick, then add to it salt and sugar, and cut good fresh bread in round sops and put the sops on it; serve it forth as a pottage. (H279 PD, 29)

Sops in Almond Milk

Take fine standing almond milk and colour it with saffron and a portion of honey; then take toasted slices of bread, and wet them in white wine or red, and put them in a dish, and boil in a little of the milk, and pour that on them, and strew on sugar and serve. (H5401, 20)

Sops in Ale with Marrow

Take marrow; put it in a pot with honey, ground pepper, ground ginger and cinnamon and ale, and mix them. Take bread; cut it in gobbets, toast them, and arrange them in dishes. See that your sauce is salted; give it a colour of saffron and serve it forth. (OP, 41)

Brewis in Lent

Take a few figs and boil them and draw them through a strainer with wine; add to this a little honey. Then toast bread, and salt it, and thus, brown and moist as brewis [similar to sops], serve them, and strew enough ground cinnamon on it at the dresser.[31] (H279 PD, 130)

---

30. The recipe is defective: we have not been told to chop or grind the meat, so the gruel could not actually be 'added' to it before it is strained.
31. An alternative version adds breadcrumbs moistened with water to the wine instead of figs, and calls for pepper, cloves, maces, and sanders instead of cinnamon.

Brewis in Summer

For 20 messes. Take one and a half pounds of almonds and blanch them and pound them in a mortar with beef broth to make a good, thick, milk, and strain it, and put it in a pot; add cloves, and mace, pine nuts, currants, and chopped ginger. Add sugar to this. Take two fillets of pork, chop them and pound them raw in a mortar. While pounding them add five egg yolks; and when it has been pounded finely take it up and lay it on a plate and add ground pepper, saffron, ground cloves and salt and mix it all together. Take a pan of fair water, set it over the fire and bring it to the boil. Make small balls of the mixture and cast them into the pan and let them boil, and when they have boiled a little while, take them out and put them in the almond milk and boil them together. When this has been taken off the flame, add a little vinegar, and if you want to change the colour in the winter time add saffron and sanders and then it will be a sanguine colour [red]. (Ar 334, 129)

Oil Sops (Onions on toast 'sops')

Take a good quantity of onions and mince them, not too finely, and boil them in clean water; take them up, then take a good quantity of stale ale, such as three gallons, and put in this a pint of good oil which has been fried, and add the onions. Let it boil together a long while, and add saffron and salt; and then put out bread in the manner of brewes and put the liquid over it, and serve it forth hot. (H4016, 130)

Pike on Sops

To make Pike on Sops, take your pike and boil it with rosemary, thyme and parsley, and make a sharp sauce with wine, water, ale and salt. Then take the contents of the pike's stomach and chop it into tiny pieces and boil it in wine and water, adding cloves, mace, ginger, cinnamon, minced dates, currants and sugar. Then cut white bread and place it on a platter and lay the pike on it and add the boiled stomach contents with the richest broth that the pike was cooked in and serve it.[32] (NBC, 160)

32. Another pike dish served on sops is listed under 'Pike in Brewet', page 76, above, and another is listed under 'Pike in Latimer Sauce', page 68, above.

Roast Chicken, a Sauce for

Take a pint of good claret wine and put in it a pennyworth of sugar and a half pennyworth of currants and set them on the fire until they boil; meanwhile cut sops of white bread and lay them on a platter, and lay the roasted chicken on them. When your wine is well boiled with the sugar and currants, take it from the fire and put in a half pennyworth of butter, cinnamon, and as much beaten ginger. And stir them well together, and pour it on your chicken and the sops. (Sl 4, PD 59)

Slit Sops (Leeks on sops)

Take the white of leeks and slit them, and put them to boil in wine, oil, and salt. Toast bread and lay in dishes, and put the sauce over it, and serve it forth. (FC, 82)

Sops Chamberlain

Take wine, cinnamon, ground ginger, sugar: of each a portion, and put it all in a strainer and hang it on a pin; let it run through a strainer two or three times, until it runs clear. Then take fresh bread and cut it as for brewes, and toast it, and lay it in a dish, and put enough white powder [recipe in Chapter 1, page 22, above] on it; then pour the liquid on the sops and serve it forth as a good pottage. (H4016, 104)

Sops Chette (False 'sops' of meat in almond milk)

To make Sops Chette, take almond milk made with fresh broth and set it on the fire to boil. Add to it cloves, mace, pine nuts, currants, minced ginger, and plenty of sugar, and in taking it off the fire add vinegar mixed with ground ginger. Then take boiled fresh boar's meat and cut it in pieces an inch square and put it in the pot, and stir it together. It should be thin; and salt it and serve it. (NBC, 21)

Sops Dorre (Golden sops)

Take ground almonds and draw them up with wine; boil it. Add saffron and salt. Take toasted bread and put it in wine; lay a layer of this and another of the sauce, and all together. Decorate it with sugar and ground ginger and serve it forth. (FC, 84)

Sops in Galantine (Accompaniment to baked lamprey)

When the lamprey has been removed, take out the galantine into a container and add wine, and mix it together until it is smooth. Add sugar, and if necessary more spice powder, and mix together so that it is somewhat thin. Then put it in an earthen pot and set it on a fire's coals until it reaches boiling, and stir it well. Have white bread cut in slices as brewes, and toast it a little, then baste it, and pour some of the galantine into the same pastry shell so that it can wet the bottom, and put some of your bread in this and pour in more galantine; then put in the rest of your bread and the rest of your galantine, and lay it on the table and serve it forth. (OP, 118)

Sops in Galangale

Take ground galingale, wine, sugar, and salt; boil it together. Take toasted bread and pour the sauce over, and serve it forth. (FC, 133)

Sops Mare (Soup of onions in almond milk)

Make good milk of almonds and make oil of almonds, and then slice onions and fry them in almond oil, and put the onion rounds on top of the milk. When you have arranged it, strew sugar on it. (DC, 58)

Jellied dishes

Jelly of Meat or Fish

To make a well thickened jelly, take white wine and a part of water and saffron and good spices, and flesh of pigs or hens or fresh fish, and boil them together. When it is boiled and cold, arrange it in dishes and serve it forth.[33] (DS, 36)

Leach (Coloured jelly, with almond milk)

For this take two sets of calves' feet and half a set of roe deer feet and boil them or scald them and pick away the hair. Then cook the feet well and discard the large bones.

---

33. Flesh of many different meats and fish were recommended for this dish, sometimes with a portion of vinegar in the liquid; the saffron is omitted for 'Crystal Jelly' (OP, 101).

Break these feet in a mortar and add almond milk, and grind this together and strain it, then set it over the fire and let it boil. Then have your pots with colours ready on the fire, and put in this jelly and stir well so that the colours will take. Then, hot as they are, ladle them into good basins as you wish.[34] (HUI, 3)

Tench in Jelly

To make a Tench in Jelly, take red wine and put it in a pan; then take your tench and scald it and split it and put it in the pan to cook. When it is done, lay it on a platter and pull off the skin and pick out the bones. Then put the skin in the liquid and set this on the fire again and let it boil. Then take good white sugar and add it to sweeten it, and add salt, saffron, ginger, and verjuice, and draw it through a strainer. Then take your tench and lay it in a platter, and put blanched almonds on it and put on the jelly, and serve it. (NBC, 277)

Pasta

Cressee

Take best white flour and eggs and make pasta dough; and in the dough put fine choice ginger and sugar. Take half of the dough coloured with saffron and half white, and roll it out on a table to the thickness of your finger; then cut into strips the size of a piece of lath. Stretch it out on a table as illustrated,[35] then boil in water; then take a slotted spoon and remove the cressees from the water. Then arrange them on, and cover them with, grated cheese; add butter or oil, and serve. (AN A, 5)

Lozenges (Lasagna noodles)

Take good broth and put it in an earthenware pot. Take flour of white bread and make a paste of it with water, and make pastry leaves as thin as paper with a roller; dry these hard and boil them in broth. Take grated rich

---

34. A similar recipe (eM, 88) uses calves' feet and bread and some ground almonds.
35. A diagram here suggests the noodles are crossed, presumably one colour over the other.

cheese and put it on dishes with mild spice powder, and lay on it boiled noodles as whole as you can get them, and put powder and cheese on top; do this two or three times, and serve forth.[36] (FC, 50)

Macrons (Macaroni, but flat)

Make a thin leaf of dough and carve it into pieces, and put them into boiling water and boil it well. Take cheese and grate it, and melted butter, put [them] above and below, like lozenges[37] and serve forth. (FC, 95)

Ravioles (Ravioli)

Take wet cheese and grind it well and mix it with eggs and saffron and a good quantity of butter. Make a thin foil of dough and enclose them as tartlettes, and put them in boiling water and boil them. Take hot melted butter and grated cheese, and lay the ravioli in dishes; lay the hot melted butter with grated cheese above and below, and put mild spice powder on it. (FC, 94)

36. 'Lozenges on a Fish Day' (FC, 132) were to be cooked in almond milk; the Lenten versions (such as H4016, 134), also known as 'Open Lozenges' (OP, 133), were simply fried in oil.
37. I.e., lasagna.

CHAPTER SIX

Meat and Game Cooked and Served other than in Pottage

Appraylere

Take the flesh of lean pork and boil it well, and when it is boiled chop it small; then take saffron, ginger, cinnamon, salt, galingale, aged cheese, and crumbled bread and grind it in a mortar; add your meat to the spices and see that it is well ground, and mix in raw eggs. Then take a long [clay] pitcher, rinsed all over; discard your grease and fill the pitcher with your meatball mix, and take a piece of good canvas and double it, and cover the mouth with this, binding it fast around the rim, and put it in to boil along with your large pieces of meat, in lead[?] or in a caldron, so it will be well cooked.

Then take up your pitcher and break it, saving your filling, and take a good spit and put it through it and put it on the fire. Then have a good batter of spices, saffron, galingale, enough cinnamon, and flour, ground well in a mortar, and mixed with raw eggs; and add enough sugar from Alexandria. And continually, while it dries, baste it with batter, and serve forth. (H279 LV, 27)

Gammon of Bacon

To make a fresh gammon of bacon without waiting, boil the salt bacon in fresh water until it is half cooked; then take it out and steep it. Set an equal amount of fresh hot water boiling in another pot, and put the bacon in the boiling water and boil it until it is soft enough. Afterwards you can flay it and serve it. (SA, 2)

Beef or Mutton Birds

Take beef or mutton and cut it like steaks. Then take raw parsley, minced onions, and yolks of hard-boiled eggs, and marrow or suet, and chop these small all together. Take ground ginger and saffron, and mix this together with your hand and put it on the meat slices all over, and salt them; then roll them up and put them on a round spit and roast them until they are done. Then lay them in a dish and pour over them vinegar and a little verjuice, and enough ground pepper, and ginger and cinnamon, and a few yolks of hard-boiled eggs crushed on them, and serve forth. (H279 LV, 30)

Beef Birds in Sauce

[Prepare beef 'birds' and roast as in recipe above.] Then take wine and cinnamon, ground cloves, and raisins; boil together. Then lay your roasted beef in dishes with ground ginger; pour the sauce over, and serve forth. (RD12, 167)

Beef Pudding

Take the blood [of an ox or a sheep] and stir it with your hand, and throw away any lumps below; then take suet of the same [beast] and mince it small, and put it into the blood; also put in plenty of oat groats, and fill up the intestines with this, and boil them. And afterwards broil them, when they are cold,[1] and serve them forth. (P1047, 14)

Beef Rolls

Take good tender beef and grind it fine, then lay it on a platter and add to it ground pepper. Then take blood of pigs or capons and add to it minced parsley, sage, hyssop, savory, and saffron, with wine, eggs, and flour – all drawn through a cloth; and boil them well together. Then make the beef into rolls; wet them in the egg mixture and put them in the broth. Boil them well together and serve them forth. (P, 224)

Beef Tongue

Take the tongue of an ox and scald it, and shave it well until it is quite clean, and boil it; and then take a spit, and lard the tongue with lardons

---

1. It is not clear whether we are to wait until they are cold before broiling them or to eat them cold; neither seems very likely.

and stud with cloves, and roast it, and when it is well roasted baste it with yolks of eggs, and serve it forth. (DS, 43)

Beef Tongue Garnished

[Prepare and cook as in the recipe above. Then] make a syrup of wine and spice powders and maces, with a little almond milk, and salt. Season it up with ground ginger and a little verjuice; colour it with turnesole. Lay the hot slices in dishes and pour the syrup over them. (RD12, 34)

Salt Beef (Corned beef)

Buy two pennyworth of beef and cut it in two. Take flour and make of it a heavy pastry; make of this a solid cake. Put a little lukewarm water into a platter; add to the water a handful of salt. That beef that you wish to have salted, prick in many places with a skewer and cover it well in the water and salt, and let it absorb the salt. Enclose it in the pastry cake. Set a pot over the fire with clean water; put in the beef, both pieces. Boil it tender. Take them both out of the pot; take away the pastry from the two pieces and lay them together, and give forth. (CCC, 12)

Beef Steaks *see* Venison Steaks

Brawn, Sweet and sour

Take parboiled dates and raisins and grind them in a mortar, then draw up your mixture with vernage[2] or clarre, or else good bastard, and let this boil well. And put in it broken cloves and sugar or honey, and ground cinnamon; and in taking it off add a little vinegar mixed with ginger and cinnamon, and colour it with sanders and saffron. In the boiling, add minced ginger. Then take fresh brawn and slice it, and put three slices in a dish; then take fried pine nuts, all hot, and put them in the pot, and pour the sauce around the slices and serve it forth. (H1605, 134)

2.   A strong, sweet wine – like the 'bastard' suggested as an alternative.

Cormarye

Take coriander, caraway ground small, ground pepper and ground garlic, in red wine; mix all this together and salt it. Take raw pork loins and flay off the skin, and prick it well with a knife, and lay it in the sauce. Roast it when you wish to, and keep the drippings which fall from it in the roasting, and boil them in a pot with good broth and serve it along with the roast. (FC, 54)

Coue de Rouncin

Take pig's feet and ears and make them clean, and boil them in half wine and half water. Add minced onions and good spices, and when they are cooked take them out and roast them on a gridiron. When it is roasted, pour over the same broth mixed with amydon and minced onions, and serve it forth. (DS, 44)

Dupercely (A boiled pork dish)

Take raw pork and discard the skin; cut it in small pieces and boil it in water until tender. Then add a portion of wine to it and let them boil well together. Take amydon or wheat flour baked with wine and blend them together; season it with salt and good spices and serve it. (P, 213)

Founet (Lamb or kid with poultry in sauce)

Take blanched[3] almonds; grind them and mix them with good broth. Take a lamb or a kid and half roast it, or a third part; chop it in gobbets and add it to the milk.[4] Take small birds, stuffed and stewed, and add to them sugar, ground cinnamon, and salt. Take hard-boiled yolks of egg cut in two and sprinkled with ground cinnamon, and decorate the top of the stew. Take alkenet, fried and dipped in wine, and colour the top with a feather, and serve it forth. (FC, 63)

---

3. 'unblanched' would appear to be a mistake.
4. The recipe forgets to tell us to cook the meat, and to add the poultry as a further touch.

Haggis

Take the guts with the tallow and parboil them; then chop them small. Grind pepper and saffron and bread, and [add] yolks of eggs and raw cream of fresh milk; put it all together and put in the belly of the sheep, that is, the stomach. Then boil it and serve it forth.[5] (H279 LV, 25)

Haggis of Almayne

Take eggs, draw them through a strainer. Parboil parsley in rich broth; cut it together with hard yolks of eggs. Add to this ground ginger, sugar, salt, and marrow, and put it in a strainer in a boiling pot; parboil it. Take it up, let it cool, and cut it small.

Take the drawn eggs and put them in a pan; make sure the pan is moist with grease. Let the batter run around into a leaf, and put on it [the] hard yolks, marrow, and parsley; turn the four sides together so that they close above and make it square. Take the same batter and wet the filled eggs so that they hold fast and enclose the stuffing; turn it upside down, fry it on both sides, and serve it forth.[6] (OP, 104)

Hare in Civy

Hares in Civy shall be parboiled, and larded, and roasted; and take onions and mince them very finely and fry them in white grease; and grind pepper, bread, and ale, and add the onions to this, and boil it. Mix it together and colour it with saffron and salt it, and serve it forth. (DS, 8)

Hare in Frissure (Hare in fricassee)

Take killed hares and wash them in beef broth with all the blood, and boil the blood and skim it well; then parboil the hares and chop them, and fry them in good grease, and put them in a pot and let them boil together. Add to this minced onions, cloves, maces, pine nuts, and currants, and dip chips of bread in wine and add them, as well as ground pepper and

5. 'Fronchemolyle' (variously spelled) is another name for haggis; recipes as titled omit the guts. 'An Entrail' (H279 LV, 21), is a variant of 'haggis': a stuffing of roasted pullets, pork, cheese, and beaten egg is baked in a sheep's stomach.
6. This, of course, has nothing to do with 'haggis'. It may or may not be of German origin.

cinnamon and sugar, and colour it with saffron. Before serving it mix in a
little vinegar, then serve it forth.[7] (Ar 334, 150)

Hare in Papdele (Smothered hare)

Take a hare and chop it in pieces; parboil it in water. Clarify the broth,
and put in your meat; boil it. Season it with mild spice powder and salt.
Take fried lozenges of pastry or wafers; arrange them in dishes and pour
the sauce over them. (OP, 30)

Hare in Talbots

Hares in Talbots shall be chopped into gobbets raw, and boiled with the
blood. Take bread, pepper, and ale and grind together, and mix it with that
same broth, and boil it and salt it and serve it forth.[8] (DS, 9)

Hare in Worts (Hare in greens)

To make hare or salt goose in greens, take a pot of good meat broth and
marrowbones and set it on the fire. Chop the hare in pieces and add to the
pot, and draw some broth through a strainer with the blood of the hare.
Take greens, the white of leeks, and other good herbs, and shred them
small together. If it is an old hare, cook it well before you add your greens,
but if it is a young hare cook them all together.

Or take a goose which has been salted for a night and a day, and chop
it into the greens in the same way. (NBC, 173)

Leach Casuay (Veal leach, but more of a pottage)

Take veal and boil it; take three or four pounds of almonds and blanch
them and grind them in a mortar, and mix them with the broth which the
veal was cooked in. Then take sugar and ground ginger and mix it together.
Put it in an earthen container, mixed with the veal broth, and serve it forth.
(Sl 1108, 102)

---

7.   A variant of this recipe, entitled 'Stuffing for Hares', without the final vinegar, appears
     in Ar 334.
8.   NBC calls this dish 'Hare in Sauce'. Other later versions put onions and ground
     almonds in the sauce.

Lombard Stew (A pork stew)

Take pork and roast it, and put it in a pot with wine, sugar, whole onions, cloves, ginger, saffron, sanders, and fried almonds. Season it with wine with ground ginger, galingale, and cinnamon, and serve it. (NBC, 188)

Mutton Birds *see* **Beef Birds**

Mutton Pudding (Blood sausage)

Take the blood and swing it with your hand, and throw away the lumps that appear; then take suet of the same and mince it small and put it in the blood. Also put in plenty of oat grits, and fill up the intestines with this, and boil them. Afterwards, broil them when they are cold and serve them forth. (P1047, 14)

Mutton Steaks *see* **Venison or Mutton Steaks**

Mutton, Breast of, in Sauce

Take roasted breasts of mutton and chop them; then take verjuice and heat it over the fire, and add to it ground ginger. Put the chopped breast in a dish and pour the hot sauce over it, and serve it forth. (H4016, 89)

Mutton, Shoulder of, in Sauce

Take parsley and onions, and mince them, with the roasted shoulder of mutton; and take vinegar and ground ginger and salt, and put them on the minced shoulder, and eat it thus. (A1439, 11)

Mutton, Stewed

Take roasted mutton, or else capons or other meat, and mince it; put it in a pot, or between two silver dishes, and put on it parsley and onions finely minced. Then add wine and a little vinegar or verjuice, ground pepper, cinnamon, salt, and saffron, and let it stew on the coals, then serve it forth. If you have no wine nor vinegar, take ale, mustard, and a quantity of verjuice, and use this instead of wine or vinegar. (H4016, 18)

Noble Roast [9] (A meatloaf with a crust?)

Boil it very well in water, and then cool it in the water. Then remove the skin with your hands and mix the fat with beaten eggs. Then take a brass mill and grind various kinds of spices: cinnamon, fresh saffron with a new savour, cloves: grind everything together. You will need plenty of eggs: the whites shall be mixed in, the yolks baked with flour [as a crust?]. This food is good for young ladies. (DC, 48)

Pig [whole] in Bars

Take a pig and stuff it and roast it, and in the roasting baste it; and when it is roasted, put over it one bar of silver foil and another of gold, and serve it forth whole to the table for a lord.[10] (Ar 334, 157)

Pig [whole] Stuffed

Take raw eggs and draw them through a strainer; then grate good bread and take saffron and salt and ground pepper and sheep's suet, and mix it all together in a good bowl. Then put your pig on a spit; stuff it and sew up the hole, and let it roast, and then serve forth.[11] (H279 LV, 33)

Pork in Almond Cream

Scald a pig; cut it into large pieces. Boil it in water and salt. Take it up, and lay it cold. Take cream of almonds; mix it well with wine and a great deal of vinegar, so that it is fairly thin. Add ground ginger and a great deal of white sugar and salt, so that it is somewhat sweet and sour. Lay the pieces in the cream and serve it forth together. (RD12, 29)

Pork in Egredouce (Sweet and sour pork)

Take fresh brawn [boar's meat or pork] and boil it and carve it into thin

9. This is a very difficult recipe: it does not even say what kind of roast is recommended. My translation is largely guesswork.
10. 'Pork in Comfit' (Ar 334, 49 and 151) is a somewhat humbler version of this, calling for rolling roasted fillets of boar's meat in either honey and wine or honey clarified with an egg before giving them the final decoration of gold and silver bars.
11. A more elaborate recipe (OP, 167) calls for cooked pork ground with figs as the basis for the stuffing.

slices, and lay three in a dish; then take dates and currants and wash them clean, and grind them in a mortar. In the grinding, add a few cloves, and draw it up with clarre[12] or other sweet wine, and put it in a pot and let it boil, and add to it a good deal of sugar or honey and minced ginger. And in the setting down, add ground cinnamon and vinegar, mixed together, and colour it deeply with sanders and saffron. Then take pine nuts or blanched almonds and fry them in good grease, then take them up and let them dry; and when you wish to serve your meat, put the nuts in the pot and pour the sauce over it and serve it forth. (Ar 334, 51)

Pork in Gole (Pork in a sweet almond milk sauce)

Take figs and raisins; grind them. Take the blood of a pig and amydon, or rice flour or bread, and ground ginger and cinnamon, and mix all this with milk of almonds. Then take honey or sugar and stir it in well, and see that it is very thick. Take the roasted pig and cut it in pieces; put it in dishes, and put on the Gole with sugar. Serve forth. (RD12, 30)

Pork in Sage Sauce

Take pigs scalded, and quarter them, and boil them in water and salt; take them up and let them cool. Take parsley and sage and grind it with bread and hard-boiled yolks of eggs; mix in vinegar, in a somewhat thick mixture, and lay the pigs in a container and the sauce over them, and serve it forth[13]. (FC, 31)

Pork, Fillets of, Endored

Take off the skin from fillets of pork and put them on a spit; roast them. Take spice powder, and baste them. Take yolks of eggs drawn through a strainer; when the fillets are roasted, dry them, so that no grease is running on them, and 'gild' them with the aforesaid yolks of eggs. (OP, 111)

---

12.   See recipe, under 'Drinks and Confections', page 187, below.
13.   Some other recipes suggest adding ginger and/or pepper – one also adds cinnamon, saffron, and honey – and cutting the meat up in smaller pieces; this is to be served cold. Other recipes, such as H279 PD, 117, suggest other meats, such as chicken, in a similar sage sauce.

Pork, Fillets of, in Galantine

Take fillets of pork and roast them until they are half done; cut them in pieces. Draw up a mixture of bread and blood and broth and vinegar, and add it; boil it well, and put in ground pepper and salt and serve it forth. (FC, 30)

Pork, Fried

Take brawn [pork or boar's meat] and cut it thin; then take the yolks of eggs, and some of the white with them, and white flour, and draw the eggs through a strainer; then take a good quantity of sugar, saffron, and salt, and add them, and take a good pan with fresh grease and set it over the fire; and when the grease is hot take the brawn and put it in the batter and turn it well in it, then put it in the pan with the grease and let them fry together a little while. Then take it up onto a nice dish and sprinkle sugar on it, and then serve forth. (H279 LV, 45)

Pork, Legs of, Endored

Put pork legs on a spit; remove the skin. Roast them; take spice powders and baste. Then take yolks of eggs drawn through a strainer; when the legs have roasted enough, dry them so that no grease runs on them, and 'gild' them with the yolks. (RD12, 214)

Pork, Legs of, in Green Sauce

Make green sauce in the best way with brown bread and subtly ground herbs, and wrap your leg in this; then take minced egg yolks, raisins, pepper and salt, and put this on your leg: and if you wish, cloves and maces. (A1393, 2)

Pumps (Boiled meatballs in sauce)

Boil a good gobbet of pork, not too lean, as tender as you can, then take it up and chop it as finely as you can; take cloves and maces and chop them with them, also chopping currants. Then take this up and roll it as round as you can, like small pellets two inches round, and lay them on a dish by themselves. Then make good almond milk and mix it with rice flour and let it boil well, but see that it is cleanly runny; and at the dresser, put five pumps in a dish and pour this pottage over. If you wish, set on each pump a wild flower, and strew enough sugar and maces on top, and serve it forth. Some people make pellets of veal or beef, but pork is the best.[14] (H279 PD, 138)

Rabbit

Take a rabbit and slay it. Draw it above and beneath, and parboil it, and lard it and roast it. Leave the head on; undo it and sauce it with ginger sauce and verjuice and ground ginger, then serve it forth. (H4016, 60)

Rabbit, Chicken or Duck

Take a rabbit, chicken, or duck and roast it until almost done, or else chop it and fry it in fresh grease; and fry minced onions, and put all together in a pot with fresh broth and half wine. Add cloves, maces, ground pepper, and cinnamon, then steep fresh bread in the same broth and draw it through a strainer with vinegar. And when it has boiled well, add the liquid to it, and ground ginger and vinegar, and season it up, then serve it forth.[15] (H4016, 63)

Rabbit in Gravy

Rabbits in Gravy shall be boiled and chopped into gobbets; and grind ginger, galingale, and cinnamon, and mix it with good almond milk and boil it. Take maces and cloves and add them, and the rabbits also, and salt them and serve it forth. (DS, 10)

Rabbit in Sauce

Take rabbits, and boil them well in good broth. Take Greek [sweet] wine and add it, with a portion of vinegar and ground cinnamon, whole cloves, whole qubebs, and other good spices, with currants and ginger, pared and minced. Take up the rabbits and cut them into pieces, and put them in this sauce, and cook them a little together, and serve it forth. (FC, 65)

14.   Another recipe adds eggs and more spices to the meatball mix, and makes the almond milk with meat broth.
15.   It is not clear whether this is more of a pottage than a roast or fried dish, nor whether it all gets mixed together in the end. An almost identical recipe is headed 'Haggis'.

Rabbit in Turbatures

Take rabbits and parboil them, and roast them until they are nearly done, and then take them and chop them into gobbets and put them in a pot. Add to this almond milk made with good broth of beef, and put in cloves and minced ginger, and pine nuts, and currants, and sugar or honey, and let it boil. Colour it with sanders or saffron, and in taking it off the fire add a little vinegar and ground cinnamon, mixed together, and serve it forth. (Ar 334, 46)

Rabbit, Two out of One

Take a rabbit; scald it clean with water, not too hot. Slit the skin from the throat to the near haunch, than take it and flay it first to the forefeet within the skin, and let it hang by [itself]. Then boil pork and [add] the yolks of hard boiled eggs. Take grated bread; also grind figs, one pound, or one pound of dates, and grind them with the pork and the yolks. Add to this ground pepper, crushed maces and cinnamon and cloves. Add honey and saffron and salt. Part this stuffing into three [parts] and colour [one] with sanders, another with saffron. Take another part: colour with green herbs.

Then fill one part of the skin and the first leg with one of the colours and another with another colour, and so forth. Lay your stuffing on endlong in another colour you have put by, and so on until you have filled it. Then sew the vent together with white thread and put it on a spit with the other [i.e., the flayed rabbit] and roast it. In the roasting, you shall colour the legs and the feet, one with alkenet, another with green herbs, another with saffron, another with turnesole or sanders. Roast and give forth with the other. (CCC, 87)

Ramioles in Egredouce (Meatballs[?] in sweet and sour sauce)

Take some pork and grind it with eggs; add currants, ground pepper, and ginger. Fry broken almonds and put all this together. Then make sauce in this way: take fresh broth and mix it with almond milk, and add saffron, sanders, good spice powders, with vinegar and sugar, then put all together on the fire mixed with eggs and sauté, and so serve it forth. (P, 101)

Veal as Counterfeit Sturgeon

Take veal hocks and calves' feet and boil them in honey. When you have boiled them tender,[16] take the bones out. If the meat is long, pound it for a stroke or two and put it in a good canvas bag and press it well. Then take it and slice it nicely in thin slices, not too broad. Take onions, vinegar, and parsley and lay them on it, and so serve it forth. (GK, 24 [Sl 1108])

Veal, Freeshe of (A ground veal dish)

Take calves' blood and boil it, and good fat, fresh and fine broth of beef; grind it with veal in a mortar and mix it with fat broth, and add white grease and good spice powder, and boil it, and dry it, and give it forth. (WW, 54)

Veal in Bukkenade

Chop veal in pieces; put it in a pot. Add onions cut roughly and herbs and good spices, cloves, maces, sugar, saffron, and salt, and boil it with a little fresh broth. Then add good cow's milk; boil it up with yolks of eggs. Let it be fairly thin, and serve it forth; and you can make it with almond milk in the same way. When it is boiled, season it with ground ginger and verjuice. (OP, 57)

Veal Loin, Larded

Take the loin and lard it with lardons and with cloves. Roast it and serve it forth. (WW, 56)

Veal, Minced in Red Sauce

Almond milk, rice flour, ground veal, diced veal added; galingale, cinnamon, sugar; the colour, sandragon red. (AN B, 6)

Veal Roast

Take good breasts of veal and parboil them, and lard them, and roast them, and then serve forth. (H4016, 69)

---

16.   The MS reading is 'all to powder', but this clearly won't do.

Venison Collops, Stewed

Take slices of roast venison and put them in a pot; add whole spices, ground spice powder and cinnamon, and a good deal of fresh broth. Season it with ground ginger and vinegar and serve it. (NBC, 190)

Venison or Beef Steaks

Take venison or beef and slice it, and grill it until it is brown; then take vinegar and a little verjuice and a little wine, and put enough ground pepper on it, and ground ginger, and at the dresser strew on enough cinnamon so that the steaks are completely covered with it, with only a little sauce, and then serve forth.[17] (H279 LV, 31)

Venison or Mutton Steaks, Stewed

Cut venison or mutton in small little slices and put them in a frying pan with ale and boil them until they are nearly tender. Then take them and fry them in butter until they are tender; then make a sauce for them. Take red wine, enough vinegar, and butter, and put them in a pot to stew until they are half evaporated; then season them with cinnamon, ginger, and sugar, and colour it with saffron. (RD12, 281)

Venison with Frumenty *see* Frumenty (Chapter 3, page 33, note)

Venison, Noumbles of (Offal)

Take the offal and wash them clean with water and salt, and parboil them; take them up and dice them. Do with them as with other offal.[18] (FC, 55)

Venison, Roast

Take good fillets, cut away the skin. Parboil them so that they are stiff throughout. Lard them with salt lard; put them on small spits and roast them. If necessary, you can baste them. Take them off and cut them in

17.   A simpler recipe (RD12, 82) makes the sauce of ginger and verjuice.
18.   See 'Noumbles', page 59, above.

broad slices. Lay them in dishes. Strew on ground ginger and salt. Handle butts of venison in the same way, and serve them forth.[19] (OP, 158)

Vertdesire

Almond milk, rice flour, chicken meat, red wine, sugar, parsley; the colour shall be green. (DC, 2)

Viande d'Espayne (Spanish dish)

Almond milk, rice flour, chicken meat, a portion of ground pistachio nuts strewed above, ground cloves put in it to give as good flavour of the pistachio nuts; the colour shall be yellow. (DC, 4)

Viande of Cypres

Almond milk, rice flour, ground ginger so that it tastes well of the ginger, and it should be strewed with gingerbread [see recipe page 191, below] and ground pistachio nuts; the colour, yellow.[20] (DC, 28)

Vinegrate

Take small fillets of pork and roast them until half done, and cut them into gobbets, and put them in wine and vinegar with minced onions, and stew it together. Add good spice powders and salt, and serve it forth. (FC, 62)

Weasels (Counterfeit 'weasels' – basically, pork)

First grind pork, and mix it with eggs and ground pepper and cinnamon; enclose it in a capon's neck, or in the stomach of a pig, and roast it well. Then cover it with a golden batter of eggs and flour to serve. (LCC, 123)

19.   'Roast Fat Venison' is more or less the same, but calls for basting with wine, ginger, pepper, and salt, with a basin to catch the droppings so they can be re-used.
20.   Later recipes have many variants, but generally contain chicken meat and/or pork. 'Viande of Cypres Bastard' contains both, plus various spices, eggs, etc.; the 'Salmon' version substitutes salmon, as does the 'Lenten' version, which decorates with pomegranate seeds. The 'Royal' version contains wine ('Viande Royal') or is served with a wine sauce.

CHAPTER SEVEN

Poultry and Feathered Game Cooked and Served other than in Pottage

Birds, Small or Large

Take ouzels,[1] thrushes, fieldfares, and all other small birds; pluck them while dry and roast them. The sauce for them is ground ginger and salt. (CUL, 157)

Bittern *see* Crane

Roast Brew (A variety of snipe)

Take and slay it in the mouth as you would a curlew. Scald it and draw it as you would a hen, and break its legs at the knee; and take away the bone from the knee to the foot as you would a heron, and cut off its neck by the body. Then roast it, and raise the legs and wings as as you would those of a heron, and no sauce but salt. (NBC, 113)

Bunting *see* Crane

Chicken Endored

Take a chicken, draw it and roast it; let the feet be on and take away the head. Then make a batter of egg yolks and flour, and add to it ground ginger and pepper, saffron and salt, and spread it over it until it is roasted enough.[2] (H4016, 71)

---

1.   Probably means a sort of blackbird.
2.   'Chicken Florished' is the same, with the addition of studding the bird with cloves and slivers of almonds.

Chicken in Brittenet (Poached stuffed chicken)

Take chickens and break the breast bones. Then take pork and chicken meat and grind them small, and mix them with broth of your meat;[3] add to this currants, broken fried almonds, ground pepper, saffron, cloves, and yolks of eggs. Season it with salt and stuff your chickens well with this, then sew them above and below; poach the chickens in fresh broth. Lay two in a dish and put sauce on them made in this way: take almond milk and put it on the fire, and add to it cloves, pepper, cinnamon, sanders, saffron, sugar, and vinegar. See that the colour is brown and yellow, and pour it on your chickens, and add maces and cubebs and serve it forth. (P, 108)

Chicken in Cassels (Two chickens out of one)

Take capons and scald them. Take a pen [quill] and open the skin at the head, and blow into it until the skin rises from the flesh, and take off the skin whole. Boil the meat of hens and yolks of eggs and good spices and make a stuffing, and fill the skin, and parboil it, and put it on a spit and roast it, and while it roasts baste it with yolks of eggs and good spices. And take the capon's body and lard it, and roast it, and take almond milk and amydon and make a batter, and baste the body with this as it roasts, and serve it forth.[4] (DS, 28)

Chicken in Caudle

Take chickens and boil them in good broth, and take them up. Then take raw yolks of eggs and mix them with the broth; add ground ginger and enough sugar, saffron and salt. Set it over the fire without boiling, and serve the chickens whole or broken, and pour the sauce over. (FC, 35)

Chicken in Cretyne

Take chickens and scald them and boil them, and grind ginger or pepper and cumin, and mix in good milk, and add the chickens to this, and boil them, and serve it forth.[5] (DS, 24)

---

3. I.e., the broth resulting from previously boiling the chicken and pork.
4. A variant of this recipe, 'Chicken in Kyslanes', RD12, 240, calls for stuffing the capon skin with ground chicken meat plus quince paste and a pine nut confection.
5. Milk is the essential ingredient for this dish, although some recipes substitute almond milk.

Chicken in Glass

Scald capons; wash them clean. Draw them, then slit them with a knife from the crop up to the neck above the shoulders. Then remove the skin with the point of a knife on both sides, from the crop to the neck. Then cut the bone apart above at the shoulders and pick out the neck bone, until you come to the head; then cut it away there at the head. Then take the skin off the capon until you come to the pinions; then flay it until you come to the second joints. Then cut off the pinions and let them hang on the skin, and when you come to the second joints then cut off the pinions and let them hang on the skin, and when you come to the legs at the knees cut the joints apart with the skin and let the foot hang by the skin. Then take a needle and thread and sew it from the crop up to the head, and leave there a little hole in the nape.

Then take a urinal[6] or a glass and put in the feet first. Then take the meat of the capon and boil it tender in a pot with some pork. Pick out the bones and the skin of the pork; chop it small and grind it in a mortar. Add to this dates; add white sugar and ginger, cinnamon and saffron and salt. Grind all together with a raw egg. Take the capon when it is in the urinal; take this stuffing, put [it] in at the neck and with a stick first fill the legs, and so upward all the body, and fill the wings and upward to the neck.

Then take a skewer and set it in the neck within the skin to hold up the head. Then fold that, whole, and set the glass in salt on a board and put it in an oven and bake it. Take it forth. Take a little alkenet; melt it with grease and put it on the head of the capon. Then set it in salt and give forth. (CCC, 86)

Chicken in Herbs

First stuff your capon with savory, parsley, and a little hyssop; then take the neck, removing the bone, and make a pudding of it with an egg and grated bread and chopped liver and heart added, with ground pepper and saffron. Then sew the large bill end firmly. Then boil your capon, with parsley, sage, hyssop, savory, and a little catmint: bruise them quickly and break in two. Put them in with slices of bacon surrounding them, and colour your broth with saffron. When it is boiled, lay it in a dish with the bacon beside the

6.   Long glass flask.

neck. Take ground saffron mixed with ale and cider to decorate your capon in the dish, and serve it then. (LCC, 112)

Chicken in Hochee (Boiled chicken with grapes and garlic)

Take chickens and scald them. Take parsley and sage, with other good herbs, and garlic and grapes, and stuff the chickens full, and boil them in good broth so that they can easily be boiled in it. Serve them and put on some mild spice powder. (FC, 36)

Chicken in Mose

Take blanched almonds and grind them small, and mix them with pure water and put them in a pot, and add to this rice flour and sugar and salt and saffron, and boil them together; and lay the yolks of hard-boiled eggs in dishes. And take roasted chickens, and take the legs and the wings and the flesh and cut that other part by length, and lay it in the dishes with the yolks; and take the sauce and pour it into the dishes, and put cloves on top, and serve it forth. (UC, 20)

Chicken in Salome

Take a capon and scald it and roast it; then take thick almond milk mixed with white wine or red, and take a little sanders and a little saffron and make a marbled colour, and so at the dresser put it on in the kitchen, putting the milk on the top, and that is most comely; and serve forth. (H279 PD, 152)

Chicken in Sauce

Take chickens and chop them for common people, but for a lord take whole chickens; boil them in fresh beef broth with a good quantity of wine. And when they are nearly done, take out the chickens. Beat eggs in a mortar with sage and parsley, and mix this with wine, and press it through a strainer, and add to it ground cloves, an ounce of sugar and an ounce of cinnamon, and a little vinegar, and colour it with saffron and salt it. Then put the chickens in dishes and pour the sauce over and serve it.[7] (NBC, 6)

7.   This sauce could be called an 'egredouce', but a very special one.

Chicken or Goose, Roast

Stuff the bird with a mixture of: the leaf of fat from the interior, parsley, hyssop, rosemary, and sage, all finely chopped together, with crumbled boiled egg yolks, currants, spice powder, saffron, and salt. Baste with the grease. When it is done, keep moist with a mixture of wine and ginger. (NBC, 125)

Chicken with Brewes

Take half a dozen chickens and put them in a pot; add to them a good gobbet of fresh beef and let them boil well. Add to this parsley, sage leaves, and savory, not chopped too small, and enough saffron. Then cut your brewes[8] and scald them with the same broth; salt it well. If you do not have beef, take mutton, but first stuff your chickens in this manner: take and boil eggs hard, and take the yolks and chop them small, and chop with them cloves, maces, and whole pepper, and stuff your chickens with this. Also put whole gobbets of marrow in. Also dress them as you would partridges, and colour them well, and lay them on the brewes, and serve them in with bacon. (H279 PD, 144)

Chicken Stewed

Take parsley, sage, hyssop, rosemary and thyme and break them between your hands and stuff the capon with it, and colour it with saffron, and place it in an earthen pot and put splinters under it so that it doesn't touch the pot. Put herbs around it and add a quart of good wine to the pot and no other liquid; then cover the pot and make a batter and seal the lid so that no air escapes. Then set it on a charcoal fire and let it stew easily.

When it is done, take it off and sit it on a straw mat so that it doesn't touch the ground; then take out the capon with a fork and put it in another pot while you check that it is done; and if it is not, stew a little longer. Then take good wine and add currants, sugar, saffron and salt to it and boil it a little, and take it off the fire and mix some powdered ginger with it. Put the capon

---

8. Also spelled 'brewis', slices of bread to be used under the meat; like 'sops', but not to be quite as soaked in the liquid.

on a platter and degrease the stewing liquid, and add the degreased sauce to the seasoned wine, and pour it over the capon and serve it.[9] (NBC, 130)

Chicken Stuffed

Take hens or young pullets and blow under the skin covering the breast. Then take stuffing made of boiled pork and grind it and mix with hard egg yolks, and add to it powdered ginger, currants, and salt. Then stuff the chicken between its flesh and the skin. And you may gild them as they roast, or make them green,[10] and serve them. (NBC, 55)

Chicken or Goose Stuffed

Take parsley and pork grease or suet of mutton and parboil them in good water and fresh broth, boiling. And then take yolks of eggs boiled hard and chop them small with the herbs and salt, and add ground ginger, pepper, cinnamon, and salt, and grapes if they are in season: if not, take onions and boil them, and when they are boiled enough, with the herbs and the suet, all together, stuff in your goose or capon, and then let it roast.[11] (H4016, 72)

Cormorant *see* Crane

Crane (Roast)

The crane shall be arranged on a spit just like a woodcock; the sauce is ginger. And bitterns and curlews shall be prepared like a crane and the sauce ginger. Cormorants shall be scalded and parboiled and larded and roasted; the sauce is ginger. Plovers, mallards, teals, larks, finches, buntings: all these shall be roasted and served with fritters and brawn; the sauce shall be ginger.[12] (UC, 15)

---

9.   'Chicken Stewed with Beef' is pretty much the same recipe, adding an equal number of pieces of beef loin, to be alternated with the chickens/capons in the pot.
10. Other recipes of this type suggest 'endoring' the chicken.
11. Other recipes for stuffing for chicken omit pork or suet and one includes bread, but they are otherwise similar. Recipes for roast chicken also give similar directions for stuffing.
12. Separate recipes for some of the birds here listed say 'no sauce but salt'.

Curlew, Roast *see* **Crane**

Doves Stuffed

Take a piece of beef or mutton, wine, and water; boil it, skim it clean. Then take doves; insert whole pepper in them and put them in the pot, and let them stew well together, and take ground ginger and a little verjuice and salt, and add them. Put them in nice dishes, a dove or two in a dish, for a sort of pottage, and when you serve it take a little broth and put it in the dishes with the doves. (OP, 105)

Duck in Civy

Take a mallard and pull it dry, and turn it over the fire. Draw it, but don't let it touch any water; chop it in gobbets and put it in a pot of clean water and boil it well. Take onions and boil them, and grind them with bread and pepper, and draw this through a cloth. Mix it with wine and boil it, and serve it forth [with the duck]. (DS, 52)

Duck in Gele *see* **Rabbit or Duck in Gele or Civy**

Duck in Sauce (Stewed or braised duck)

Take chopped ducks [13] & boil them in fresh broth, and add cloves, mace, pine nuts, sugar, and minced onions. Then mix into the pot crumbs of bread soaked in wine, and add ground pepper, and let it boil. Colour it with saffron and sanders, and salt it, and when you take it off the stove add a little vinegar and serve it. (NBC, 36)

Duck, Roast

Break the neck of a duck; pull it dry and draw it as you would a chicken. Cut off the head, the neck, the wings, and the feet. Roast it. (OP, 152)

Egret, Roast

Take a egret; slay it as you would a crane, scald it and draw it and cut its wings, and fold its legs as you would a crane's, and roast it and serve it

13. Wild ducks are specified in all duck recipes: usually, as here, mallards.

forth; and no sauce but salt. Raise the legs and the wings[14] as those of a heron, and no sauce but salt. (H4016, 52)

Finch *see* **Crane**

Goose in Hochepot

Scald them well and cut them into gobbets raw; cook them in their own grease and add a cupful of wine or ale. Mince onions finely and add them to this, and boil it, and salt it and serve it forth.[15] (DS, 22)

Goose in Porre (Salt goose in leek sauce)

Take a goose and split it [so that it will lie flat], and wash it, and salt it, and let it lie all night; and in the morning wash it clean and chop it, and put the meat in a pot with fresh broth and set it on the fire. Then take the white of leeks and grind it in a mortar, and as you are grinding it add oatmeal, and put this in the pot and let it boil, and colour it with saffron, and salt it, and serve it.[16] (NBC, 34)

Goose in Sauce Madame

Take sage, parsley, hyssop and savory, quinces and pears, garlic and grapes, and fill the goose with these; sew the hole so that no grease comes out and roast it well, and keep the grease that falls out. Take galantine[17] and grease and put in a pot. When the goose is roasted enough, take it off and cut it in pieces, and take the stuffing and put it in a pot, and add wine to it if it is too thick; add ground galingale, mild spice powder and salt, and boil the sauce, and arrange the goose in dishes and put the sauce on top.[18] (FC, 32)

---

14. Which you have already been told to cut off; all versions seem to have this illogical contradiction.
15. Many recipes add water in the first step here; some add herbs and/or spices, bread, and blood.
16. See 'Hare in Worts', page 98 above, for a variation on this recipe adding greens.
17. See below, in Chapter 10, Sauces and Condiments, page 148.
18. Some recipes make the droppings the basis of the sauce, and perhaps that is what we are supposed to do with the galantine-thickened droppings here. A simpler version of this stuffing/sauce, consisting of parsley, grapes, and garlic roasted in the goose, then ground with hard yolks of eggs and verjuice, is in A 1439.

Goose, Roast *see* **Capon or Goose, Roast**

Goose, Stuffed *see* **Chicken or Goose, Stuffed**

Goose, Wild *see* **Swan or Wild Goose**

Heron

The heron shall be prepared as the swan is, if it comes to the kitchen live. The sauce for it shall be made as a chauden is, with ginger and galingale, and it shall be coloured with its blood or with toasted crusts.[19] (UC, 13)

Lark *see* **Crane**

Mallard *see* **Crane, Duck**

Partridge in Saracen Sauce

Take partridges and roast them. Then take fresh grease and put it in a pot, and add currants and dates, cut small, and let it fry together. Then draw up almond milk with wine and put in it ground cinnamon, cloves, long pepper, sanders, saffron, sugar, and vinegar. Then put your partridges and all together into the pot and heat it again, then serve it forth. (P, 100)

Partridge or Woodcock, Stewed

To stew partridge or woodcock, draw the bird and wash it; stop them with whole pepper and put them in an earthen pot, and add minced dates, currants, wine, and fresh broth. Salt it and boil it, and when it is done season with ground ginger and verjuice. Colour it with saffron, salt it, and serve it. (NBC, 196)

Partridge *see also* **Peacocks and Partridges**

Peacock in Hauteur

Take a peacock and break its neck. Blow it [under the skin] so that the skin and the feathers rise from the flesh, all whole, with the tail; then roast it and serve it forth in its feathers, and pick off the skin under the breast

19.   Some recipes recommend ginger sauce for a roast heron; one in OP calls for ginger, vinegar, and mustard.

and set it on a shield, and spread its tail abroad. Serve it as if it were a live peacock. (CUL, 141)

Peacocks and Partridges

Peacocks and partridges shall be parboiled and larded and roasted, and eaten with ginger. (DS, 3)

Petydawe (Fried goose oddments)

Take the waste parts of young goose – the heads, the necks and the wings, the gizzard, the heart, the liver. Boil it well and lay it on a board. Cut the wings at the joints and the feet from the legs and every claw from the other. Cut the gizzard, the liver, and the heart in long slices. Have good white grease hot in a frying pan and put in all the meat and fry it a little, and add to it ground pepper and a little salt. Have yolks of eggs drawn through a strainer, and pour into the frying pan; when it is slightly hard, turn it. Fry it through, but not too much: enough to hold it together, and serve it forth. (OP, 165)

Pheasant, Roast

Let a pheasant bleed in the mouth like a crane, and let it bleed to death; pull it dry, and cut away the neck and the head by the body and the legs by the knee, and put the knees in by the vent, and roast it. Its sauce is sugar and mustard.[20] (H4016, 46)

Pigeons, Roast

Take pigeons and pull them dry, and cut off the heads and the feet; draw them, roast them. Sauce for them is ground pepper, vinegar, parsley, and onions minced small. (CUL, 154)

Plover see Crane

Quail, Roast

Slay a quail; lard it and roast it as a partridge. Raise its legs and wings as of a hen, and no sauce but salt.[21] (OP, 144)

20.   The recipe in OP disagrees: 'No sauce but salt'.
21.   Another recipe recommends cameline sauce.

Snipe, Roast

Slay it as you do a plover; pull it dry. Let the neck be whole except the wings. Let the head be on: put the head to the shoulder. Fold its legs as you did a crane; cut off the wings. Roast it and raise its legs and wings as a hen, and no sauce but salt.[22] (OP, 154)

A Summer Dish

Take giblets of capons and of hens and chickens and doves, and make them clean, and boil them, and cut them small; and take parsley and chop it small, and arrange it all in platters. Pour vinegar on it and put on ground ginger and cinnamon, and serve it forth cold at night. (Ar 334, 41)

Swan or Wild Goose

Take a swan and cut it in the roof of the mouth; keep its blood to colour the chauden. Or else knit its neck, scald it, and roast it as a goose, and the sauce for it is chauden. (CUL, 136)

Swan's Feet in Sage Sauce

See Pork in Sage Sauce, page 101 above, for the sauce used for this dish. (NBC, 237)

Teal *see* Crane, Duck

Woodcock, Roast

Slay it as you would a snipe; pull it dry. Or else break its back and keep its skull whole. Draw it as you would a snipe; put the bill through the thighs. Roast it; raise the legs and the wings as of a chicken, and no sauce but salt. (OP, 155)

Woodcock, Stewed *see* Partridge or Woodcock, Stewed

---

22. The directions about wings are puzzling, but other versions of this recipe are puzzling in other ways.

CHAPTER EIGHT

Fish Cooked and Served other than in Pottage

Boiled Barbel

Take a barbel[1] and cut it and draw it in the nape as you would a round pike, and boil it in water and salt, ale, and parsley. And when it comes to a boil, skim it clean and put the barbel in it, and boil it. Its sauce is garlic or green sauce; and then serve it forth. (H4016, 169)

Bass, Mullet or Bream

Draw all these at the belly. Scale them clean with the edge of a knife; wash them. Make the broth of water and salt; when it boils, skim it clean, and slit the fish across the side and put it in the boiling broth, plus sage and parsley; and serve it forth somewhat hot. Serve the bass and the mullet with ginger sauce and the bream with garlic. (OP, 179)

Braised Fish

Take dace,[2] trout, and roach, and roast them on a griddle, then boil them in wine; put verjuice on it, ground ginger, and galingale, and bring it in. (H279 PD, 76)

Boiled Bream or Roach

Take a bream or a roach and scald it in water, and draw it in the side by the head, and notch it with a knife in the side in two or three places, but not through; and boil it in water, ale, and salt, and serve him forth hot; the sauce is verjuice sauce or ginger sauce. (H4016, 160)

---

1.   A large European freshwater fish.
2.   A freshwater fish related to carp.

Roast Bream in Sauce

Scale a bream; draw him in the belly and prick him two or three times in the backbone, roast him on a gridiron. Take wine; boil it and add to it ground ginger and verjuice, and put the bream on a dish, and pour the sauce over it. (OP, 171)

Bream *see also* Stuffed Pike or Bream; Braised Tench or Bream

Chysanne

Take roaches, whole tenches, and plaice, and chop them into gobbets. Fry them in oil. Blanch almonds; fry them, adding currants. Make a thickener of bread crusts with red wine and a third part of vinegar; add cut-up figs, strong spices, and salt. Boil it. Lay the fish in an earthen pan and put the sauce over it; boil minced onions and add them to this. Keep it, and eat it cold. (FC, 106)

Codling, Haddock and Hake, Boiled

To prepare cod, hake or haddock, take and slit them at the belly, and cut them from side to side in round pieces, and if using large haddocks, cut off the head and make a large tail to serve to your sovereign. Make the sauce of water and salt, and when it boils, skim it clean and put in the fish and the liver. Add parsley and let it stand in the sauce until you serve it hot.[3] (NBC, 139)

Stuffed Codling's Head

Take the liver of the fish and boil it, then take bread and steep it in the broth, and grind the liver and the bread together; add to this ground ginger and cinnamon and saffron, and add a little of the broth and currants and cloves and maces, and mix it well together. Put it in the head and make it fast, and boil it well, and serve it forth.[4] (Ar 334, 116)

3.   The OP recipe adds ling to the fish in this list, and suggests garlic for the sauce, as does H4016, RD12 adding green sauce as an alternative; but OP says haddock should be served cold with ginger sauce.
4.   A simpler recipe, but one that does not specify how it is cooked, is 'Tavorsay' (L553, 19) for codling's head and liver, bones removed, seasoned with pepper and ginger.

Conger in Pyole

Take almond milk made with conger broth. Add clarified honey or sugar, cloves, maces, pine nuts, and currants, and boil it, and colour it with saffron. In setting it off the fire, add ground ginger mixed with verjuice. Then take pieces of parboiled conger and broil them, and arrange them in dishes, and pour on the sauce. Then sprinkle your pottage with turnesole and serve it. (NBC, 43)

Conger in Sauce

Take the conger and scald it and chop it in pieces, and boil it. Take parsley, mint, pellitory, rosemary, and a little sage, bread, and salt, strong spice powder, and a little garlic, a little cloves; take this and grind it well. Draw it up with vinegar through a cloth. Put the fish in a container and pour the sauce over, and serve it forth cold. (FC, 107)

Conger in Service (Roast)

Take conger; scald it, shave it clean, and draw it clean. Leave the belly whole. Wash it; split it along the bone. Prick the body with slivers of almonds and cloves; roast it and baste it with ground cinnamon and wine. Keep the droppings, and baste it with them again until it is roasted enough. Grind almonds; mix them with fresh fish broth and wine. Put in a pot with ground pepper, minced dates, and sugar. Boil it up, and season it with ground ginger, vinegar, and salt, so that it is somewhat sweet and sour.

Chop the conger into pieces of whatever length you wish; put it on a platter. Pour the sauce over it. See that it is coloured with alkenet. Make a garnish of minced pared ginger and anise in comfit and sweet spice powder, and strew it on. (RD12, 90)

Conger, Turbot, Halibut, Boiled

Scale a conger, not in hot water, for fear of breaking. Cut off the head and if you wish you may split him. Cut your conger a little before the navel in the belly, so that you may loosen the gut. Take it out at the throat, and the liver and the entrails at the gut. Cut the belly crosswise in round pieces; ensure the hair has been shaved away from the back and the belly right to the tail, and the whole fish should be shaved clean so that the skin is not broken and thoroughly white. Draw your turbot by the fin beneath the gill and cut off the head, and separate the white side from the black and cut off the gills with a knife on both sides. If your turbot is large, split it down lengthwise and if it is little cut it crosswise and along the ribs, backbone and all. Cut the halibut in the same manner and plunge it in fresh water and keep it white, make a sauce with fresh water and if you do use any salt let it be but a little. When it boils, skim it clean. When the conger is cooked enough, take it up with a skimmer and lay it in a vessel with fresh water and salt, and have ready another vessel of fresh water and salt, and when the turbot and halibut are boiled pour out the broth and put in a little cold water and take up the fish with your hand to guard against breaking, and lay it in water and salt. Serve two or three pieces of conger on a platter for the lords and strew with sprigs of parsley; and serve the rest to the other men, with green sauce. Lay the turbot and the halibut on two of the broadest platters and pour over green sauce and strew with sprigs of parsley. (OP, 180)

Crab or Lobster

Take a crab or lobster: stop it at the vent with one of its little claws; boil it in clean water and no salt. Or else stop it in the same way and put it in the oven, and let it bake, and serve it forth cold. Sauce it with vinegar. (OP, 170)

Dory in Service [5]

Draw the dory at the gill so that it is clean. Take the liver, or the liver of haddock or codling; chop it in small pieces, with parsley, and grated bread and good spice powders, salt, and saffron. Make a good stuffing and put it in at the gill; prick it in front so that the stuffing will not go out. Lay it on a roasting iron and roast it slowly and long. Lay trenchers of bread, if it is necessary, around the body to prevent the breaking out of the stuffing.

---

5.   John Dory, a European fish.

Take some of it boiled and draw through a strainer with wine and the fat of the broth that the liver was boiled in,[6] and add a great deal of cinnamon. Boil it up; season it with ground ginger and verjuice so that it is somewhat sour. Salt it and lay the dory on a platter and pour the sauce over it. If you wish, chop it in pieces when it is roasted, and treat it the same way, and serve forth. (RD12, 86)

Eel in Comfit

Take eels and flay them and cut them into thin gobbets, and fry them in olive oil, with pine nuts. Take these and arrange them in white powder[7] and sugar, and put on top as much ground ginger as the number to be served requires. Then take blanched almonds and grind them small and mix them with white wine; strain them, and cast everything into a pot, and take ground cloves, maces, cubebs, and pepper, and boil all of this together, and salt it. And when it is arranged for serving, decorate it with minced ginger that has been well pared and selected. (UC, 1)

Eel in Sorre

Wine, water, fresh eels and other kinds of fish; the eels fried, the mixture loose, the pieces dusted with ground cinnamon; colour, red.[8] (AN B, 19)

Eel Reversed

Flay large eels; flay off the skin until you almost come to the tail. Shave away all the hairs; split it along the back as you do a conger. Leave the belly whole; remove the bone. Take the skin of another eel; make sure it is clean and split its length. Roll it in ground grains of paradise and wine or verjuice, and a little saffron and salt. Lay it within the body of the eel; lay the whole eel together again. Prick it full of cloves and pine nuts and pared ginger, and slide the skin over it all. Bind it fast at the head so that the moisture will not go out. Put it on a spit and roast it. See that the body

6. A step we were not informed of before.
7. See recipe, page 22, above.
8. Most recipes do not call for frying the eels and colour the dish with sanders: the name apparently means 'in red sauce'. But most late versions are actually variants of 'Eel in Brewet' and omit red colouring.

within it is basted with the syrup described above and wash it in hot water before it is put on the spit.[9] (RD12, 216)

Eel Reversed Stuffed with Herbs

Take thyme, parsley, sage, and all sweet herbs, with onions and herbs minced, pepper, saffron, chopped yolks, and raisins in your stuffing; and when it is roasted[10] pour a little vinegar on it. (A1393, 32)

Eel, Baked

Take eels and place them in a dish and sprinkle them with salt and saffron and ground pepper, and cover the dish with another dish and set it on the coals; and turn the dish around, and put in a little wine the first turn to save the container, and put the hot coals in a hole in the earth, and so let it boil, and serve it forth. (H5401, 63)

Flounder *see* Superpusoun

Gurnard, Boiled or Roasted

Take a gurnard and draw it in the belly, and save the stomach, and boil it in a good broth as you do a pike, and serve it with green sauce or ginger sauce.[11] If you want to roast it, split it from the tail through the back and the head and roast it on a gridiron; then take all the contents of the gurnard's stomach and boil it in a broth sharpened with vinegar and wine, and draw this through a strainer, and add to this ground ginger, saffron, and salt, and let it boil together. And when your gurnard is roasted enough, put it on a platter and put the sauce on it, and so serve it forth. (P, 130)

Haddock, Boiled *see* Codling, Haddock and Hake

9. A simpler recipe in A1393 does not tell us how to 'reverse' the eel, but does remember to tell us to 'draw' it and includes a more elaborate stuffing, adding minced dates, currants, minced onions, and chopped egg yolks. It also calls for a different 'syrup' for seasoning the body of the eel, in a separate recipe, which follows; and another stuffed reversed eel follows that.

10. As in the recipe above.

11. Other recipes suggest vinegar and pepper.

Haddock in Civy

[The fish] shall be opened and washed clean, and boiled, and roasted on a griddle. Grind pepper and saffron, with bread and ale; mince onions, fry them in ale, and add them, with salt. Boil it; put your haddock on platters and your civy above, and give forth.[12] (L553, 20)

Hake, Boiled *see* Codling, Haddock and Hake

Halibut *see* Conger, Turbot, Halibut, Boiled

Lamprey, Fresh or Salt, in Galantine

Open it at the navel and let out a little blood, and gather that blood in a container, and discard the gall. Scorch it well, and wash it well, and make a pastry dough and put the lamprey in it with good spices; then make a layer of bread mixed with wine or vinegar, and mix the blood with this, and put in raw galantine[13] a towel over it and set it in the oven until it is baked; and if it is roasted, prepare it in the same way except that you cook the galantine with onions. And if the lamprey is salt, wash it in hot water and in wheat bran, and after that put it in hot water all night, and on the next day scorch it and boil it well with onions; and make the galantine by itself, since the lamprey should be served cold and the galantine hot by nature.[14] (UC, 24)

Ling, Boiled *see* Codling, Haddock and Hake (*note*)

12.   This recipe is typical, but a variant in OP, duplicated in NBC, departs from the norm by including no onions in any form: probably in error, since onions are the basis of a 'civy'.

13.   Meaning the bread thickening for a galantine sauce?

14.   Some recipes for 'Lamprey in Galantine' omit bread; many call for salt lamprey. 'Roasted Lamprey' calls for roasting on a spit, with a galantine of wine, onions, spices, etc.; the onions being conspicuous here, it is sometimes called 'Civy of Lamprey'.

Ling, Civy of

Take ling and cut it in pieces and roast it on a spit, and when it is roasted enough put it in a good pot. Fry minced onions and currants in good oil and put this in with almond milk drawn with good fish broth, then add ground pepper, ginger, salt, saffron, and vinegar. Boil it a little and serve it forth. (P, 208)

Loach *see* Minnows or Loach

Lobster *see* Crab or Lobster

Luce in Soup[15]

Parboil the luce; then take onions and mince them and fry them in grease, and add wine and saffron; [the luce] and all kinds of fish, for best results, should be fried without grease in the manner here described. Take an egg yolk or two and rub the [hot] pan until it appears to sweat; the pan should be quite black and wiped thoroughly with a cloth, and should be carefully watched lest it become too hot or too cold. Sprinkle with a little salt or sugar on [the surface of] the pan; [fry the fishes] as you would serve them on a plate, putting in one after the other without letting them touch each other; then serve. (AN A, 12)

Mackerel, Boiled Fresh

Draw a mackerel at the gill; save the belly whole. Wash it; make your sauce of water and salt, and if you wish you may add ale. When it boils, put in parsley and mint leaves and add your fish to this; serve it forth hot, and sauce it with verjuice. (OP, 185)

Mackerel in Service

Draw the mackerel; wash it, roast it. Make a sauce of ground ginger and wine and vinegar, and mostly ground cinnamon. Boil it up; lay the mackerel in dishes and pour the sauce over. (RD12, 88)

---

15. This is a puzzling title: no 'soup' or sauce is specified, and 'sops' do not seem appropriate. But perhaps it is a general recipe for how to cook fish to go into a soup.

Mackerel, Stuffed

Draw a mackerel at the gill, then lay the mackerel on a board on an apron.[16] Beat it lustily with the edge of your hand, from the gill to the tail continuously. Then with a round roll begin at the tail and roll upward on the fish at the gill and at the sides. Break the bone at the tail a little from the base, but do not break the skin. Also break the bone at the nape and at the gill, and draw the bone out softly at the gill. The fish that hangs [on the bone?] strike off with the other fish.

Take salmon from the thickest part of the fish and an eel. Boil the salmon and the eel tender. Add to the fish of [for?] the mackerel hot boiling water; take it up from the water. Strip the eel and lay the salmon and all the other fish without bones in a mortar and grind it together with a little grated bread. Add to this ground ginger, cinnamon and saffron and salt, mixed together, and with this stuffing stuff the mackerel with a little stick. Then lay it on a gridiron on a reed or two and roast it, and turn it often, and give forth. (CCC, 5)

Minnows or Loach, Boiled

Take minnows or loach and pick them over, and make sure of a good quantity of ale and parsley. When it almost at the boiling point, skim it clean and add the fish to it, and let it boil. If one wishes, add a little saffron to it, and the sauce is green sauce. Then you shall serve them forth hot. (H4016, 104)

Mullet, Boiled, Roast or Fried

Scale a mullet and draw it in the belly and boil it in water and salt, and serve it hot or cold with green sauce; or else scale it and roast it raw on a gridiron, and make sauce as for a boiled sole and put it on it; or else fry it in good oil. (D55H, 148)

Mullet *see also* **Bass, Mullet or Bream**

16. Most medieval aprons were large squares of cloth, without bibs. Thus an apron would have been a handy cloth, larger than a napkin or a towel, to cover a kitchen surface.

Perch, Boiled

Take a perch and draw it in the throat, and make it a sauce of water and salt; and when it begins to boil, skim it and put in the perch and boil it. Serve it forth cold, and put on it leaves of parsley, and the sauce is vinegar or verjuice. (H4016, 157)

Pike in Brasee (Braised pike, grilled, plus sauce)

Take pikes and undo them in the belly and wash them clean, and lay them on a roasting iron. Then take good wine and ground ginger and sugar, a good deal, and salt, and boil it in an earthen pan, and serve the pike with the sauce over it. (FC, 110)

Pike in Galantine

Take brown bread and steep it in a quart of vinegar and a pint of wine for a pike, and a quarter ounce of ground cinnamon; and draw it through a strainer quite thick and put it in a pot, and let it boil. Then add to it ground pepper or ginger or cloves, and let it cool. Then take a pike and boil it in good liquid, and take it up and let it cool a little, and put it in a bowl to carry it in, and put the sauce under and above it, so that it is all hidden in sauce; and carry it wherever you wish.[17] (H4016, 152)

Pike in Pickle [18]

Draw pikes; scale them clean with the edge of a knife. Wash them, dry them with a cloth. Lay them on a roasting iron on a good charcoal fire; roast them. Take the stomach contents of the pike, and of other pikes, and boil it. Take it off; chop it small and put it in an earthen pot with cloves and mace, ground cinnamon if you have it, minced dates, currants. Boil it up together with the fat of the drippings and wine and a little sugar. If you wish, mix ground cinnamon and pepper with the wine and add it. When it is boiled, season it with ground ginger and verjuice and a little finely ground mustard, and draw it through a strainer. Lay the pike on a platter and pour the sauce over. (RD12, 76)

17. Another recipe call for adding fried minced onions, hot, which seems dubious considering that all recipes call for cooling the fish.
18. A 'pickle' was a sauce with mustard in it.

Pike in Sauce (Fried pike in an almond milk sauce)

Split pikes; chop them in pieces and parboil them. Take them up and pick out the bones. Fry them. Grind almonds and draw them up with wine. Fry onions finely minced, and add them, with cloves, mace, and good saffron and salt. Put the hot fried pike in dishes and pour the hot sauce over.[19] (RD12, 80)

Pike in Worts (Pike with vegetables)

Split a pike; parboil it in fresh broth of fresh fish. Take it up and remove the skin. Pick out the bones; leave the pieces whole. If you wish, you may fry it. Grind almonds and draw up with the aforesaid broth; put the milk in a pot. Take fresh parsley and other good herbs, and onions; parboil the herbs and press out the water. Chop them small and add to the milk. Fry raisins a little and add them, and boil it, and add sugar and the contents of the fish's stomach finely cut. When it has boiled enough put in the pike, and dress as vegetables, with the pike lying in them. Make a garnish of pared ginger minced finely and anise in comfit and white powder: strew this over it. (RD12, 37)

Pike, Stuffed

Take the pocket of the pike and wash it clean, and scrape the pike and wash it clean, and take the liver of the pike and chop it small and grind it well, and add to it ground galingale and ginger and cloves, salt and saffron; fill the pocket full and boil it well, and serve it forth. (H5401, 19)

Stuffed Pike or Bream

Take a pike and splat him in the back and draw out the refet;[20] then take the bowels, make them clean and boil them. Then chop the …[*text not clear*] and the swimming bladder and grind them with the liver and the bowels; add cloves, galingale, ginger, pepper, saffron, and salt, with sugar

19. 'Pike in Worts' (RD12, 37) adds to this dish several herbs, fried raisins, and the contents of the pike's stomach, minced. 'Pike Reversed' (RD12, 79) is not reversed at all: it is like this recipe except that the sauce is made from the contents of the pike's stomach boiled in wine and fat from the fish.

20. Contents of the stomach.

and currants. Then fill the pike with this stuffing and close it up; boil it in a good broth, and serve it forth. (P, 212)

Plaice in Civy [21]

Take plaice and cut them in pieces and fry them in oil; draw a mixture of bread and good broth and vinegar, and add to it ground ginger, cinnamon, pepper, and salt, and colour it with gaudy green – and see that it is not too thick. (FC, 115)

Plaice in Sauce

Draw the plaice; chop off the heads and the fins. Wash them and dry them with a cloth. Lay small sticks on a roasting iron so that the fish will not touch the iron; lay the plaice there and roast them on both sides. Blanch almonds; draw them with the broth of fresh fish and wine. Add spice powders and salt; boil it up and season it with ground ginger, verjuice, and a little sugar. Lay the plaice hot in dishes and pour the sauce over. (RD12, 85)

Plaice, Boiled

Take a plaice and draw it in the side by the head; and make sauce of water, parsley, salt, and a little ale, and when it begins to boil, skim it clean and put in the fish and let it boil. Sauce for it is mustard and ale and salt, and serve it forth hot. Or else, take a plaice and draw it; prick it with a knife to keep it from breaking as it fries, and fry it in hot oil, or else in clarified butter. (H4016, 162)

Plaice *see also* **Chysanne**

Porpoise, Stuffed

Take its blood and grease and oatmeal, and salt and pepper and ginger, and mix these together well; then put these in the gut of the porpoise and let it boil gently, not hard, a good while. Then take it up and broil it a little, and then serve forth. (H279 LV, 40)

---

21.   'Civy' is an onion sauce, but this sauce contains no member of the onion family – in either example of the recipe.

Ray in Sauce

Take rays and clean them and put them to boil. Pick them clean and fry them in oil. Take almonds and grind them and draw them up with water or wine; add to this whole blanched almonds, fried in oil, and currants. Boil the mixture, grind it finely, and add to it ground garlic and a little salt and verjuice, strong spice powder and saffron, and boil it together. Lay the fish in a container and put the sauce over it, and serve it forth cold. (FC, 108)

Ray, Boiled

Take a ray and draw it in the belly and cut it in pieces, and boil it in water and no salt, and serve it forth cold. Its sauce is verjuice, or liver with mustard; and boil the liver with it, and serve it forth. (H4016, 163)

Roach, Boiled *see* Bream

Roach *see also* Chysanne

Salmon, Fresh, Boiled

Take it and remove the backbone; boil it in water, salt, ale, and parsley, and boil it enough, and serve it forth cold. Sauce for it is green sauce in the right time of year, or else vinegar, ground ginger, cinnamon; or else chauden, made of its own kind.[22] (CUL, 159)

Salmon, Broiled

Take the backs of fresh salmon and broil them on a gridiron, and make a sauce of vinegar, ground pepper, and cinnamon, and serve them forth. Pour the sauce over.[23] (CUL, 162)

Shrimp

Take live shrimps; pick them clean. Make your sauce of water and salt and put them in. Let them boil only a little; pour away the water and lay them

22. Another recipe (H4016, 153) suggests roasting on a gridiron before boiling, and decorating with branches of parsley dipped in vinegar, as does another. 'Noble Salmon' (DC, 50) appears to suggest a sauce made out of the ground bones of the salmon, but I am not sure I understand the recipe correctly.
23. Other recipes add ginger and minced onions to the sauce.

to dry. When you shall serve them forth, lay them in dishes all around the sides of the dishes, and lay the backside outward, and every course until you come to the middle of the dish within. Serve them forth; sauce them with vinegar. (OP, 186)

Braised Sole

Flay soles; draw them. Roast them so that they are done; lay them in dishes. Make a braising sauce as you did for the bream,[24] except for cloves and maces, and pour it on and serve it forth. (OP, 174)

Sole in Civy

Take soles and flay them; boil them in water. Chop them in pieces and remove the fins. Take boiled onions and grind the fins with them, and bread; draw it up with the same broth. Add strong spice powder, saffron, clarified honey, and salt. Boil it all together. Broil the soles and arrange it in dishes; pour the sauce over and serve forth. (FC, 122)

Sole, Boiled, Roast or Fried

Take a sole and remove the head and draw it as you would a pike, and flay it. Make sauce of water, parsley, and salt and when it begins to boil skim it clean and let it boil enough. If you want to have it in sauce, take it when it is boiled, or else take it raw and draw it, and scale it with a knife, and lay it on a gridiron and broil it. And take wine and ground cinnamon and let it boil a while, and add to it ground ginger and verjuice; put the sauce on the sole in the dish and serve it hot. Or else take a sole and remove the head, draw it and scald it, and prick it with in knife in various places to prevent the breaking of the skin, and fry it in oil or in clarified butter. (H4016, 164)

Sturgeon or Turbot, Boiled

Draw a turbot or a sturgeon and chop it, and cut them in broad pieces; boil them in water and enough salt, and serve them forth cold, a piece or two in a dish with green sauce; and put parsley leaves wet in vinegar on them. (D55A, 11)

24. See the recipe for braised tench and bream, below, but add vinegar and verjuice as a last step.

Sturgeon in Broth

Take good fresh sturgeon and chop it in water, then take it off the fire and strain the broth into a pot; pick the fish clean and add to it ground pepper, cloves, maces, and cinnamon. Then take good bread and steep it in the same liquid, and add that, and let them boil together; add saffron, ginger, and salt and vinegar, and then serve it forth. (H279 PD, 38)

Superpusoun (Flounder in a sweet sauce)

Boil raisins and figs in wine or ale; grind them, and bread with them. Add pepper and cinnamon; colour it with sanders. Put pine nuts among them, and dates cut in length. Add currants, and take flounders: cut them and flour them and fry them, arrange them in dishes and the sauce above. (RD12, 165)

Tench in Brasee (Tench in 'braising' sauce, cold)

Take a tench and nape it, and slit it in the back through the head and tail and draw it, and then make a sauce of water and salt. When it begins to boil skim it clean, and put in the tench and boil it. Take it up and pull off the skin and lay it flat, with the belly upwards in a dish. Then take parsley and onions and chop them small together; add ground ginger and put it in vinegar. Put it all on the tench in the dish, and serve it forth cold.[25] (H4016, 175)

Tench in Civy (Tench in onion sauce)

Take a tench and scald it, roast it. Grind pepper and saffron, bread and ale, and mix it together; take onions, chop them and fry them in oil, and add them, and serve it forth.[26] (H279, 95)

Tench in Egredouce

Take tenches and let them bleed. Split them flat. Boil salt and water; put these tenches into the water and boil them. Then make galantine in this

25. This sauce is similar to that described in 'To Boil a Tench', H5401, 19; most recipes of this title call for a more elaborate, highly spiced, sauce, and do not suggest serving the fish cold. As it stands, the recipe is almost identical to 'Tench in Sauce', H279, 96.

26. Two of the other recipes for this dish substitute dried fruits for the onions, and are therefore not proper 'civy' recipes.

way. Take good bread; put it in a mortar, grind it with some sanders and saffron. Mix it with good vinegar. Mince onions small, and parsley with them, then currants, and mince dates small. Put all this in the galantine, and also ground cinnamon and salt. Sweeten it with honey. Lay your fishes on dishes; pour this syrup over, and give forth. (CCC, 42)

Tench in Gravy

Splat your tench and boil it with crumbled bread, and mix it with ground pepper and saffron mixed with the tench broth. Then lay the tench on a platter and pour on the gravy, and serve it.[27] (NBC, 259)

Tench in Sylico

Take tenches and salt them, and cut those that hang by the skin, and boil them. Then take good sweet wine, or red wine with sugar, and currants picked over and washed clean, and grind it with chips of bread and with cloves, and draw it up with the same wine, and set it over the fire and let it boil. Add ground grain of paradise, and colour it deeply with sanders and saffron; in setting it down, put in verjuice and ground ginger and cinnamon. Lay the tenches in dishes and pour the sauce over, and serve it forth. (Ar 334, 197)

Braised Tench or Bream

Splat tenches in the back; take away their entrails and make them clean, and dry them with a cloth. Lay them on a gridiron. Take a great deal of ground cinnamon and draw it through a strainer with red wine. Add ground ginger, cloves, mace, sugar, and sanders, so that it is thick with ground spices. Set it on the fire; when it is near the boiling point put your tenches in dishes, the bone side up, and pour the braising sauce over them.

Scale bream in fresh water; draw them and treat them in the same way. Or else boil them in water and salt and pull off the skin; lay them in dishes splatted, and chop onions and parsley. Add ground ginger, then put all that in vinegar and pour it on the tench, and serve forth cold.[28] (RD12, 78)

27. This recipe omits the step of roasting the parboiled fish.
28. The recipe for the cold boiled fish in a sauce seems to apply to the tenches – although perhaps also bream; it is really a separate recipe, and not a 'braised' dish at all.

Tench, Roast

Take a quart of wine and a little vinegar and tender bread, and steep it all together, and draw it through a strainer and let it boil. Add ground pepper to it. Take a tench, and split it, and roast it on a gridiron; put its sauce over it in the dish, and then serve it forth hot. (H4016, 176)

Tench *see also* Chysanne

Trout, Boiled

To boil a trout, take and slice it at the head and make a sauce of water, salt and parsley, and when it begins to boil, scale it and slice it open at the belly. And cut two or three notches on the back and score it three times next to the head, and boil it. And serve it with cold green sauce and parsley leaves; or else, boil the stomach as you do with a pike and mince it and add to the cooking liquid and add powdered ginger and serve. (NBC, 131)

Turbot, Roast, in Sauce

To make Turbot Roasted in Sauce, cut away the fin of the turbot and make it into fillets, and put it on a round spit, and as it roasts sprinkle on salt. Then take verjuice, vinegar, or wine, ground ginger and a little cinnamon, and sprinkle them on while it roasts. Set a dish or pan underneath to catch the drippings, and baste it with them. And when it is roasted pour the sauce on the fish in the dishes and serve it. (NBC, 199)

Turbot *see also* Sturgeon or Turbot; Conger, Turbot, Halibut, Boiled

Whelks, Boiled

Take whelks and put them in cold water, and let them boil only a little. Take them out of the container and pick them out of the shell, and pick away their horn, and wash them and rub them well in cold water and salt, in two or three waters. Serve them cold, and put on them leaves of parsley wet in vinegar. The sauce for them is vinegar. (H4016, 180)

CHAPTER NINE

Eggs and Dairy Dishes

Allumells (Omelettes)

Break eggs into a container; beat them well, and draw them through a strainer. Then boil pork, one pennyworth for thirty eggs. Then take the lean part and chop it small on a board. Take herbs and chop them small. Then chop yolks of hard-boiled eggs; put the meat and the herbs and the yolks on a platter and add to them ground ginger and salt.

Then take a frying pan set over the fire. When it is hot wet it with a little grease on a few feathers, then add a little saffron to the eggs, and with a saucer put some of it into the pan and let it run out across the bottom. Then put on some of the topping that you have made [i.e., the chopped mixture now in the platter], sprinkling a little. Then fold the first side and the other to meet it, and overlap the ends, and take them up with a spatula and lay in a container.

Then boil figs in a pot with wine or ale or with fresh broth, then grind them in a mortar. Break raw eggs; add the yolks to the figs, then draw them through a strainer with fresh broth or wine. Put this mixture in a pot and add to it currants and clarified honey, ground pepper and cinnamon, saffron and salt; boil it on the fire and stir it well. If it grows too thick, thin it with broth of fresh meat or wine or good ale. Arrange these omelettes on a dish; pour this syrup over and scatter cinnamon above.

A pound of figs and six eggs are enough for eight dishes. (CCC, 11)

Armanack

Push raw cream through a cloth or a strainer into an earthen pan. Take whole yolks of eggs and leave them in the sun until they are hard, then take them in your hands and add them to the cream, and season them with ground ginger and cinnamon and salt. (Sl 7, 19)

Caper Viaund

Take earthen pans, and in them put the rennet of a calf and the milk of a cow, all hot, over it, and let it stand in the sun until it is set. Then put it in different containers and give it different colours; give each enough white powder[1] then put each colour by itself in a canvas. Then fold the canvas four-square, and press them with a heavy piece until they are stiff. See it is salted enough. Then slice them and scatter ground ginger above and beneath. (Sl 7, 22)

Clonnenonne

Grind figs and dates and a little boiled pork, with the figs and dates dry. Mix them with a few eggs so that the mixture is somewhat firm; add to it ground cinnamon, saffron, and salt. Gather it up into a container. Boil eggs hard; put them in cold water and then peel them clean. Then take away the yolks and make the area where the yolks were larger and put your stuffing therein, and fill them full. Then grind the yolks with raw eggs, not including the strains, and add flour, ground cinnamon and saffron and salt; make a stiff batter of this. Gather sage leaves with the small stalks. Then set grease over the fire. They lay the sage leaves over the stuffing in every half egg; dip all together into the batter and fry them, and give forth. (CCC, 77)

Cream Bastard

Take a great heap of eggwhites and put it in a pan full of milk, and let it boil; then season it with salt and a little honey and let it cool, and draw it through a strainer. And take fresh cow's milk and mix this with it, and season it with sugar, and see that it is poignant[2] and sweet; and serve it forth as a pottage, or a good baked dish,[3] whichever you wish. (H279 PD, 151)

---

1. Recipe in Chapter 1, above.
2. This word generally implies the judicious use of a sour ingredient, such as vinegar or verjuice; but none is mentioned in this recipe.
3. This may refer to its place on the menu (late in the meal), since it is certainly not baked or sliced.

Cream Boiled

Take cream of cow's milk and yolks of eggs and beat them together well, and put it in a pot, and let it boil until it is very thick; add sugar and colour it with saffron, and arrange it in slices, and put on them borage flowers or violets. (Ar 334, 108)

Doth

Take cow's milk, and mix it with wastel bread, and colour it with saffron; put in pepper and ginger and cloves, and boil it with hard-boiled eggs, and boil it with honey and sugar, and serve. (H5401, 22)

Eggs in Cocker

Take eggs; gather out the whites and the yolks from a hole made at the top end. Keep the shell. Make stuffing as you did for the Gosnade. Fill the shell with this and set the shell upright in salt. Also make the same batter that you made for the bordering of the Gosnade.[4] Take good grease and put it in a frying pan over the fire; take the eggs and dip the shell in this batter and set them upright in the grease and fry them a little, and give forth. (CCC, 75)

Eggs, Pench of

Take water and put it in a pan on the fire and let it boil; then take eggs and break them and put them in the water, and afterward take a cheese and carve it into four parts, and put it in the water. When the cheese and the eggs are well boiled, take them out of the water and wash them in clean water. Take wastel bread and mix it with cow's milk, and put it on the fire, and then season it with ginger and cumin and colour it with saffron, and mix it with eggs, and enrich the sauce with butter, and keep the cheese out; put the sauce in a dish and put the eggs on it, and carve your cheese in little slices and put them in the sauce with the eggs, and serve it forth. (DS, 38)

Eggs, Poached

Take eggs, break them and boil them in hot water, them take them up, as whole as you can. Then take flour and mix it with milk, and add sugar or

4.   Recipe on page 179, below, but, like this recipe, it is far from clear.

141

honey and a little ground ginger, and boil it all together and colour it with saffron. Lay your eggs in dishes and pour the sauce over, and add enough ground spices; white powder[5] is best. (H279 PD, 101)

Elat (Egg custard with the herb elena campana)

Take elena campana[6] and boil it in water; take it up and grind it in a mortar. Mix it with eggs, saffron, and salt, and put it over the fire, but do not let it boil; put sweet spice powder on it and serve it forth. (FC, 80)

Haggis of Almayne (German omelette[?][7])

Take eggs and put them through a strainer. Parboil parsley in rich broth; chop it together with hard yolks of eggs. Add to this ground ginger, sugar, salt, and marrow, and put it in a strainer in a boiling pot; parboil it. Take it up and let it cool; cut it up finely. Take the strained eggs; put them in a pan and see that they are moist with grease. Let the batter run around into a leaf and arrange thereon [the] hard yolks, marrow, and parsley, and turn the three sides together so they close above, and make it square. Take the same batter and wet the eggs that hold it together, and close the stuffing therein. Turn it upside down; fry it on both sides, and serve it forth. (OP, 104)

Hanoney (Scrambled eggs with onions)

Draw the white and the yolks of eggs through a strainer; then take onions and shred them small. Then take good butter or grease, barely covering the pan therewith, and fry the onions; then put the eggs in the pan and break the eggs and onions together, and then let them fry together a little while. Then take them up and serve them forth all broken together on a nice dish. (H279 LV, 49)

Herbelette (Herb omelette)

Take parsley, mint, savory and sage, tansy, vervain, clary, rue, dittany, fennel, and southernwood; chop them and grind them small. Mix them

5. See recipe on page 22, above.
6. The root of the herb elecampane.
7. 'Haggis' has nothing to do with the usual meaning of that word, and is probably a corruption of 'eggs'.

with eggs. Put butter in a pan and pour in the filling, bake it and serve forth.[8] (FC, 180)

Junket

Take fresh milk; put it through a strainer into a pan. Warm it; add to it a little rennet, and then take it over the fire and stir it together, and cover it. Then take a rush the length of it and flat, and around this rush braid another, [with] rushes crosswise as thickly as you may. Then lay these braided rushes on a plate; put the curd on top, and pour out the whey. Then turn it upside down on another plate and sprinkle above [a mixture of] sugar and ginger, and give forth. (CCC, 10)

Lete Lardes ('Larded milk')

Take fresh milk and put it in a pan. Take eggs with all the white and beat them well and add them, and colour it with saffron, and boil it until it becomes thick; then strain it through a colander, and take what is left and press it on a board, and when it is cold lard it, and cut it into slivers, and roast it on a gridiron and serve it forth. (DS, 25)

Malasade (Omelette with bread added)

Take the yolks and whites of eggs together and draw them through a strainer; and then take a little butter and put it in a good frying pan, and when the butter is hot take the strained eggs and add them. Then take a saucer and gather the eggs together in the pan, to the breadth of a pewter dish; then put good pieces of bread downward in the pan, then take it out of the pan and put good white sugar on it and serve forth. For every malasade take 12 eggs, or more. (H4016, 82)

Papins (Thickened, sweetened milk: 'pap'[?])

Take milk and flour; draw it through a strainer and set it over the fire, and let it boil a while. Then take it out and let it cool. Take yolks of eggs drawn

8. Note that some of these herbs are not in wide culinary use today; most recipes for this dish allow for far fewer, parsley, sage, and hyssop being the most usual. Some recipes add meats and fruits: a version of this variant, baked in pastry cases, is called 'Herbelette Open' (OP, NBC).

through a strainer and add them to it; then take a good quantity of sugar and add it, with a little salt, and set it on the fire until it is somewhat thick, but do not let it boil fully, and stir it well.

Pour it on a dish, and serve it forth runny.[9] (H279 PD, 20)

Pochee (Poached eggs in sauce)

Take eggs and break them into scalding hot water, and when they are cooked enough take them up. And take raw yolks of eggs and milk and beat them together, and add to them ground ginger, saffron, and salt; set it over the fire, and do not let it boil. Take [the] cooked eggs and put the sauce over them, and serve it forth. (FC, 92)

Posset (Milk curd)

Put cow's milk in a pot over the fire, and when it is boiling put in wine or ale, and no salt. Take it from the fire and cover it; as soon as the curd is gathered, take it up with a saucer or a ladle. Serve it forth, and strew on ground ginger.

If you wish, you may take the same curd and lay it on a board and press out the whey, and draw it two or three times through a strainer with sweet wine; add ground ginger and sugar, and mix it well together, and serve as a thick pottage for supper.[10] (OP, 130)

Sawgeat (Eggs with sage, with an optional sausage)

Take sage; grind it and mix it with eggs. Take a sausage and carve it into gobbets and put it in a pot with grease, and fry it. When it is fried enough, add the sage with eggs; do not make it too hard. Add mild spice powder and serve it forth. If it is an Ember Day, take sage, butter, and eggs, and let the sage be prominent, and serve it forth. (FC, 169)

Tansy Cakes

Take good tansy and grind it in a mortar; then take eggs, the yolks and the whites, and strain them through a strainer, and also strain the juice of the

9.   The recipe in H5401 uses this as a sauce for fried eggs.
10.   The second part of this recipe is given separately as 'A Pottage on a Fish Day' – no relation to the recipe of that name listed in Chapter 3, above.

tansy, and mix them together. Take good fresh grease and put it on the fire until it melts, then pour your mixture on it and gather it together with a saucer or a dish, as you wish, more or less; and turn it in the pan, then serve it forth.[11] (H279 LV, 56)

Towers

Make a good thick batter of yolks of eggs, with enough marrow, ground pepper, maces, cloves, saffron, sugar, and salt, and if you wish a little boiled pork or veal, chopped; then take the white of eggs and strain them into a bowl. Put a little saffron and salt in the white, and set a pan with grease over the fire, and be careful that the grease is not too hot; then put a little of the white mixture in the pan, and let it spread around as you make a pancake. Then, when it is somewhat stiff, put your mixture of the egg yolks in the middle, and cover your cake round about, and enclose it foursquare; fry it up and serve it forth for supper in summer. (H279 LV, 64)

11. 'Tansy in Lent' (CUL, 180 and SA, 7) was to be made with fish roe instead of eggs and oil for frying.

CHAPTER TEN

Sauces and Condiments

Black Sauce for Roast Chicken

Take capon liver and roast it well. Take anise and grains of paradise, ginger, cinnamon, and a small crust of bread, and grind it small, grinding it with verjuice and capon grease. Boil it and serve it forth.[1] (FC, 141)

Black Sauce for Duck

Take bread and blood, boiled, and grind it, and draw it through a cloth with vinegar. Add to it ground ginger and pepper and the duck's grease. Salt it; boil it well and serve it forth. (FC, 145)

Broiled Fish, Sauce for *see* Eel Reversed, Sauce for

Cameline Sauce

Take currants and nut kernels and crusts of bread and ground ginger, cloves, and cinnamon; grind it well together and add salt. Mix it with vinegar and serve it forth.[2] (FC, 149)

Chauden

Take of the swan or wild goose the gizzard and the entrails; slit them and shave them clean, and when the wings and the feet have been boiled, pick away the bones; chop it all small and put it in a pot, and boil it in the same broth and draw up a thickening of bread with red wine and mix this in. Season it with ground pepper, ginger, and salt; colour it with its own blood or with sanders so that it is brown. Take out the small bones of the feet and

1.   This sauce is entitled 'Best Sauce for Roast Chicken' in LCC, 63.
2.   The essential ingredients of this sauce were bread, cinnamon, and vinegar or wine: all others vary from one example to another.

leave the skin whole, and lay a foot in a dish and pour the chauden over it, and serve it forth.[3] (CUL, 137)

Chicken or Pheasant, Sauce for

Take almonds and grind them, and mix them with wine, and make a good thick milk; colour it with saffron and put it in a pot, and add to it plenty of pine nuts and currants and ground ginger and cloves and galingale and cinnamon, and let it boil, and add sugar to it. And when the capons or pheasants are roasted, pour the sauce over them and serve it forth. (Ar 334, 74)

Eel Reversed, Sauce for

Take fish broth and brown bread and make your liquid, and treat it as the syrup of your pestel, and lay your eel in there round.[4] (A1393, 31)

Garlic Pepper Sauce *see* Pepper Sauce for Veal and Venison (*note*)

Garlic Sauce for Roast Beef

Take brown bread; cut it in slivers and toast it until it is somewhat brown. Soak it in vinegar and put it in a mortar with a great deal of ground cinnamon, ground pepper and garlic, and only a little of the bread, and grind it well together. Put it through a strainer so it is as thick as mustard, and salt it. (RD12, 42)

Galantine

Take crusts of bread and grind them small. Add ground galingale, cinnamon, and ginger, and salt it; mix it with vinegar and draw it through a strainer, and serve it forth. (FC, 142)

---

3.   Chauden was also a recommended sauce for wild duck, pork, veal, and fish; the fish version generally called for the liver and the stomach, plus roe for a female, with bread and ale or wine. The pork and veal versions were apt to call for accompanying fried pastry pellets: see, e.g., 'Greynes', RD12, 186.
4.   This sauce is also recommended for broiled fish.

Gaudy Green (A green sauce for fish)

Take the stomach and liver of haddock, codling, and hake, and of other fishes; parboil them. Dice them small. Take the same broth and wine; make a thickener of bread, of galantine [5] with good spice powder and salt. Put in the fish and boil it, and add cumin to it, and colour it green. (FC, 97)

Gauncele for Goose (Yellow garlic sauce)

Take garlic and grind it small, with flour and saffron and salt; mix it with cow's milk, boil it well, and serve it forth. [6] (FC, 146)

Ginger Sauce

Take white bread and pare it well, and dissolve it in vinegar. Grind it and mix it with vinegar and with ground ginger and salt; draw it through a strainer and serve forth. (FC, 143)

Gravy (Broth thickened with almonds)

Take capons or fat hens and boil well; take the broth and cool it. Take almonds; blanch them and grind in a mortar and mix with the broth. Take mace, cubebs, and sugar, and put them in this milk, and take young chickens or rabbits and boil them well; remove the skin and put them in the milk, heat it, and then serve. Make fish gravy in the same way, using luce and bream. [7] (AN A, 29)

Green Sauce

Take parsley, mint, garlic, a little wild thyme, and sage; a little cinnamon, ginger, pepper, wine, bread, vinegar, and salt; grind it small with saffron and serve it forth. [8] (FC, 144)

Murree (Mulberry sauce)

Take mulberries and grind them in a mortar and wring them through a cloth, and put them in a pot over the fire; add bread and white grease, and

5. Like a galantine?
6. 'Gauncele' for chicken adds egg yolks.
7. 'Gravy Enriched' (DS, 79) adds boiled eggs and cheese, as well as spices.
8. 'Brown Green Sauce' (FC, 148) omits thyme and spices and adds pellitory and dittany, both sharp-tasting roots, and calls for verjuice or sorrel instead of vinegar.

do not let it boil more than once. Add to it a good portion of sugar, and if it is not coloured enough grind [more] mulberries, and serve it forth.[9] (DS, 37)

Mustard, Lombard

Take mustard seed and wash it, and dry it in an oven. Grind it when dry; push it through a strainer. Clarify honey with wine and vinegar, and stir it [the mustard and the liquified honey] well together, and make it thick enough; and when you wish to use some of it, thin it with wine. (FC, 150)

Parsley Sauce

Take parsley and grind it with vinegar and a little bread and salt, and strain it through a strainer, and serve it forth. (A1439, 14)

Pepper Sauce for Veal and Venison

Take bread and fry it in grease; draw it up with broth and vinegar. Add ground pepper and salt and set it on the fire. Boil it and serve it forth.[10] (FC, 139)

Pepper Sauce, Sharp

Take the grapes from the root and put them in a mortar with a little salt and crush the grapes well, and then take out the juice, and put in the mortar ginger, pepper, and a little bread, and grind together well into a powder; mix this with the juice of the grapes. (DC, 39)

Pickle

Take the droppings of well-roasted capons with wine and mustard, and onions shredded small and cooked in grease; mix all together and serve it forth. (LCC, 72)

9.   Some recipes for this sauce are simply almond milk (plus rice flour) coloured red to imitate mulberries.
10. Another version of this sauce is simply titled 'Sauce for Veal and Venison', and adds ginger. 'Garlic Pepper Sauce' is identical, but without broth, and with crushed garlic added in the second step.

Pickle for Duck

Take onions and chop them small and fry them in fresh grease, and put them in a pot. Add fresh beef broth, wine, ground pepper, cinnamon, and the duck's droppings, and let this boil together a while. Then take it from the fire and add a little mustard and ground ginger; do not let it boil further, and salt it, and serve it with the duck. (H4016, 36)

Pickle for Pork

Take half a pint of good ale, a spoonful of honey, and a spoonful of mustard and cream[?], a small morsel of bread and an apple minced finely, and set it all on the fire, and let them cook together until it is thick, and thus it is good.[11] (SA, 4)

Pigeons, Sauce for

Take parsley, onions, garlic, and salt, and mince the parsley and onions fine and grind the garlic, and mix it with enough vinegar; and mince the roasted pigeons and pour the sauce over them, and serve it forth. (A1439, 10)

Pike, Sauce for [12]

Take the contents of the pike's stomach and mince it finely and put it in a dish. Take a good portion of mustard, and put a pint of the best and fattest of the broth in the saucer and shake it, and put it into the dish with the stomach contents; and put in a little vinegar and a little verjuice and a great quantity of cinnamon and sugar and a little ginger, and as you taste it you may always amend it. (P1047, 27)

Pork Leg, Sauce for (1)

Take the broth of the pork and make your thickening with bread, then the onions, minced, and boiled with them vinegar, ground pepper, cloves, maces: boil all these well together and colour it with saffron. Wrap your leg of pork in this, and scatter above chopped yolks of eggs.[13] (A1393, 1)

---

11. These three examples illustrate the fact that a medieval 'pickle' was a rich sauce containing mustard and (usually) wine, not what we call a 'pickle' today.
12. This is a variety of 'Pickle'.
13. This sauce is also recommended (A1393, 33) for veal and other pork.

Pork Leg, Sauce for (2)

Take good wine and mix it with raw yolks of eggs; let them boil together for a while, then put ground pepper on it, and see that it is sharp with pepper. Take cloves, maces, and saffron and add them; at the dresser pour your sauce over your pork leg, and crush hard yolks of eggs on it and serve it forth. (H279 LV, 32)

Roast Duck, Sauce for (1)

Take onions and mince them well and put some in the duck; mince more onions with the duck's fat, then boil it; add ale, mustard and honey and boil until done.[14] (P1047, 28)

Roast Duck, Sauce for (2)

Take bread and boiled blood and grind them together, and draw this through a cloth with vinegar. Add ground ginger and pepper and the duck's grease; salt it and boil it, stir and serve. (A1439, 19)

Sage Sauce *see* **Pork in Sage Sauce** in Chapter 6 (page 101), above, for the most usual Sage Sauce

Salad[15]

Take parsley, sage, green garlic, spring onions, onions, leeks, borage, mints, scallions, fennel, town cresses, rue, rosemary, purslane: rinse and wash them clean. Pick them over. Pluck them small with your hand, and mingle them well with raw oil; lay on vinegar and salt and serve it forth. (FC, 78)

Saracen Sauce

Take blanched almonds and fry them in olive oil, then grind them well in a mortar and mix them with thick almond milk, and with wine and one third part sugar; and if it is not thick enough, mix in rice flour or amydon,

14. This is evidently derived from the rhymed recipe in LCC; an almost identical recipe appears in eM57.
15. This is neither a sauce nor a condiment, but as the only medieval dish which needs no cooking, it does not fit in any of the other categories.

and colour it with alkenet[16] and boil it. And when it is arranged for serving decorate it above with pomegranate.[17] (UC, 16)

Sardeynes

Take almonds and make a good milk with rice flour, saffron, ginger, cinnamon, maces, cubebs; grind them small in a mortar and mix them with the milk. Then take a nice container and a good part of sugar and boil them well, and rinse the dish all over with sugar or oil, and then serve forth.[18] (H279 PD, 99)

Sauce Madame *see* **Goose** in Chapter 6 (page 116), above

Sauce Rous

Take bread and broil it on the coals and make it brown, and lay it in vinegar and let it steep. Then take pepper, cinnamon, and nutmeg and a few cloves and put it all in a mortar, and take the bread out of the vinegar and grind it with this. When it is ground enough, mix it with wine and vinegar and draw it through a strainer. (A1439, 7)

Sauce Sylico

Scald the crane; draw it. Take the entrails and the gizzard and the heart; slit it and make it clean, and the entrails of a capon, and the grease with it. Put it all in a pot; boil it with fresh broth until it is tender and the broth is almost boiled away. Take it up and chop it small and put it in a pot with the fat of the broth and red wine, a great deal of ground cinnamon, and ground pepper and saffron. Boil it together so that it is thin and clear of the grease. Season it up with ground ginger, vinegar, and salt; and roast the crane. Serve it forth. If necessary, put some of the drippings of the crane in the sauce; serve it forth in a dish with the crane.[19] (OP, A.1)

16. In England, the preferred colour of a 'Saracen' dish was red.
17. One of the parallel recipes has a corrupted title, 'Samfarayn', W115; another adds rose hips, FC, 86.
18. There is no indication what this sauce is for; the 'sardines' apparently in the title are unlikely.
19. There are also recipes for serving tench in a slightly simpler version of this sauce.

Sauce without Fire

Take four pounds of almonds and lay them in water overnight and blanch them, and in the morning grind them well and draw up a thick milk; then take rice and wash it clean and grind it well, and draw it up with the milk through a strainer, and put it in a bowl. And divide it in the container, and put in all white sugar, and in every container cloves, maces, cubebs, and ground cinnamon; and let one part be white, another yellow, and the other green with parsley. And lay a slice of each one in a dish, and see that the milk is mixed with wine, and the other with red wine.[20] (H279 PD, 78)

Sober Sauce

Take raisins; grind them with crusts of bread and draw them up with wine. Add good spice powders and salt and boil it. Fry roaches, soles, or other good fish; pour the sauce over and serve it forth. (FC, 134)

Sorrel Sauce

Take sorrel, wash it, grind it; put a little salt in it and strain it, and serve forth. (A1439, 13)

Swan, Sauce for

Take the giblets and odds and ends and the liver of the swan and boil them in good broth; when it is boiled, take out the bones and chop the meat small. Make a thickening of breadcrust and the swan's blood and add ground ginger and cloves to it, also pepper and wine, and salt, and boil it well. Put in your meat, all chopped up, and serve it forth.[21] (LCC, 66)

Syrup (Onion sauce for roast beef)[22]

Take beef of the loin and slice it nice and thin; take minced onions and

---

20. This last direction is not very clear, but the wording in the only other version of this recipe (NBC, 60) doesn't help here: it is at least clearer in telling us to divide the original 'milk' into three bowls.
21. The usual recommendation for swan was chauden, which uses some of the same components as this sauce.
22. 'Syrup' generally means simply 'sauce', and is usually so translated here, as in 'Leg of Pork, Sauce for', for 'Siripe for a Pestel of Pork' (A1393, 1 and H279 LV, 32); but this

ground pepper and suet, and put them on the beef and roll it well, and put it on a spit and roast it brown. Take broth of fresh meat, then, and mix it with bread and minced onions, with ground pepper and cloves, and boil all together; then take boiled blood and strain it through cloth, and colour the sauce with this. Take your roast and slice it neatly the length of a finger; boil it in the sauce, and serve them together in a dish. (LCC, 101)

Veal, Sauce for *see* Pork Leg, Sauce for *(note)*

White Sauce for Boiled Chicken

Take blanched almonds and grind them all to dust; mix it with verjuice and ground ginger, and serve it forth. (FC, 140)

---

particular sauce has no further name, so its original name has been retained. No sugar is implied by the use of 'syrup': note that neither of the sauces for a pork leg contain sugar or honey, any more than this sauce does.

CHAPTER ELEVEN

Baked Dishes

Apple Tart

Take good apples and good spices and figs and raisins and pears, and when they are well ground colour it with saffron and put it in a tart shell, and put it forth to bake well. (DS, 82)

Brie Tart

Take a crust an inch deep in a container. Take raw yolks of eggs and soft cheese, and mix the cheese and eggs together. Add ground ginger, sugar, saffron, and salt. Put it in the crust; bake it and serve it forth. (FC, 174)

A Fig Tart

[Begin by making the fig mixture listed under Pottage Royal in Chapter 3, page 45, above.] To the other part, add sugar, ginger, cinnamon, and currants; mix them well together. Then make pastry with raw cream, form pastry shells, and set them in a hot place in the sun. And when they are stiff, put your stuffing in them, and stud them with cloves, and strew on white powder[1] and salt. (Sl 7, 12)

Pear Tarts

Make good tart shells; then take pears, and if they are little put three in a shell, and pare them clean, and between every pear lay a gobbet of marrow; and if you have no little pears, take big ones and cut them up, and thus put them in the oven for a while. Then take the mixture you use for Doucettes[2] and pour it in, but let the marrow and the pears be visible, and when it is done serve it forth. (H279 VF, 13)

---

1. Recipe in Chapter 1, page 22, above.
2. See Douceties, below. Basically, beaten eggs with milk and honey.

Veal Tarts

Take the kidneys of a calf with the suet and some of the meat with it, boiled until tender. Chop it small and put it in a container. Mix it with cream of cow's milk, sugar, and good spices, and ground cloves, saffron, and salt, and put it in tart shells and bake it. (P, 137)

Fish Tarts

Take flour, almond milk, and saffron, and make four spikes of this and fry the spikes in oil. Then take almonds and draw a thick milk; take maces, cubebs, rice flour, cinnamon, and galingale. Then take haddock, crayfish, perches and tenches and boil them; when they are boiled take the fish from the bones and grind it fine with your spices, and make your filling of this. When it is made, separate it into four parts, one part white, another yellow, the third green, the fourth made black with figs, raisins, and dates. Take the first portion of your fish and put your onion sauce over the fish in four quarters, like a checkerboard as broad as your pastry, and sprinkle over it sugar of Alexandria, and a spike on top. Take another portion and lay it on your four quarters as broad as your spike, and your sugar above. Take the third portion of your fish and lay on the four quarters, and put sugar over it, and a spike. Take the fourth portion like the others, gathered together, and above a hole like that of a rose.[3] (H279 VF, 13)

Lamprey or Salmon, Baked

Take lampreys and scald them with hay; and make good pastry, and arrange two or three lampreys on it, with ground ginger and pepper, and let it bake. And slice salmon in good broad pieces and bake them in the same manner.[4] (H4016, 146)

---

3. These directions may not seem entirely clear, but they are clearer than those of the preceding directions for a meat version (H279 LV, 12), made with chicken and pork.
4. Most 'Baked Lamprey' recipes are for larger pie shells and require somewhat more elaborate preparation, with the lamprey curled up in the shell: for the basic preparation, see 'Fresh Lamprey', in Chapter 8, page 127, above. This version is interesting in telling us to scald the lamprey with hay: no doubt explaining the otherwise mysterious title 'Lampray Hay' (CCC, 22).

Lamprey Tarts

Take lampreys and strip them with a cloth and boil them in water with salt and vinegar, and sprinkle them well with spice powder and salt, and put them in tart shells. And take a thick almond milk and mix it with good water or with fish broth and add spice powder, sugar and parsley leaves, vinegar and salt, and set them in the oven filled, and serve them. (NBC, 103)

Cold Tarts

Grind raisins, and if you wish you can boil figs and grind them with the raisins; and dilute them with sweet wine, as thick as you can make it. Add cloves, maces, pine nuts, currants, minced dates, sugar, and salt; set it on the fire. Stir it well; when it boils, take it off. Have small tart shells with low rims already baked and make the rims gold with saffron, and fill them with the syrup. Decorate them with anise in comfit, and if you wish to you can take walnut kernels: pick off the skin and make them as clean and white as you can. Wet them in a little saffron water. Set a pin or a needle in them and hold them upright in your hand – do not let them be too wet – and lay on gold foil with the other hand with a tool made for this purpose, and blow on them gently with your mouth, which will make your gold adhere. Thus you can gild them all over, and decorate your tarts with them. And you can thus decorate any cold tarts. (OP, 138)

Royal Tarts

Make small tart shells, and take boiled chicken or boiled pork, chopped small, or use both of them. Take cloves, maces, and cubebs and chop them with the meat; mix this with crumbled marrow and add enough sugar, then put it in the shell, and in the middle put a bit of marrow and enough sugar around it, and let it bake; and this is for suppers. (H279 VF, 33)

Dried Fruit Tarts

Take figs; grind them dry with osay wine[5] and add cinnamon, sugar, and currants, and mix them together well. Then make your pastry with raw

5.   A sweet Alsatian wine.

cream and sugar, and make tart shells and set them in the sun in a hot place; [and when they are baked,] put your stuffing in the shells and insert cloves in it, and sprinkle over enough sugar mixed with mild spices, and serve it forth. (eM, 26–27)

Small Meat Tarts

Take and boil calves' feet as tender as you can and pick away the bones, and take the meat and grind it small in a mortar, and add to it good broth and honey and a little pepper ground with grated bread, and let it all boil together. Add a few small dates to it, or raisins or ground figs; take it up and make nice tart cases filled with this, and let them bake a while, and serve them forth. (eM, 75)

Small Custard Tarts

Take raw cream and raw yolks of eggs without any white, and blend together with your hands, and make handsome small tart shells, and put in an amount that seems best to you; and put on a saffron fringe to colour it, and other good spices to make it more delicious, etc. (eM, 66)

Pork Custard Tarts

Take pork loins and boil them, and grind them a little in a mortar. Add to them a few yolks of eggs, and remove the filling and put it in a clean container and colour it with a little saffron, and add ground ginger or pepper. Make tart cases as you would to contain custard. Then take the filling and make of it pellets the size of walnuts, and lay six of them in a pastry case, or as many as you wish, and put into the same pastry case quartered dates, if you wish, and currants and maces. And take cream, and thick milk and strained yolks of eggs added to the cream, and colour it with saffron, and add sugar or clarified honey and half a saucerful of verjuice; and put the tarts into the oven, and immediately pour the syrup over them, and let them stand until they are baked. (Sl 7, 9)

Bream Pasty

Scale the bream; draw out the gall from the liver and let all the rest of it stand. Wash it and dry it with a cloth, then score it with a knife end to end from the tail to the head, to the bone in three or four places, on both sides. Take ground pepper and cinnamon and galingale. Take a pint of vinegar; add to it a little honey and the spices and saffron and salt, and a minced onion. Then make a cake of pastry. Wet the bream well in this sauce so that it absorbs the sauce; fold the cake [over the bream]. Bake and give forth. (CCC, 55)

Chewettes

Take the flesh of pork and cut it into pieces, and chickens with it, and put it in a pan and fry it; and make a pastry shell as for a small pie and put this in it, and put on top hard yolks of eggs, ground ginger and salt. Cover it and fry it in grease, or bake it well, and serve forth.[6] (FC, 193)

Chicken Pie

Take chickens scalded clean; truss them as short as you can. Colour them with verjuice [mixed with] saffron and good spices. Put them in pastry shells; take salt pork lard diced small and mixed with verjuice, saffron, and salt, and put this in the shells. Close them and bake them and serve them forth. (OP, 126)

Bordeaux Pie

Take chickens or pullets and enclose them in pastry, and add marrow chopped small, and let it bake until tender. Open the middle of the pastry above with a little hole and put into this a good quantity of egg yolks and household wine, beaten together; and blend it together without further heat, and serve it forth. (Royal)

Crustade (Custard tart)

Take a pastry case and bake it dry; then take marrowbones and put the marrow in. Then take hard-boiled egg yolks and grind them small, and mix them up with milk; then take raw egg yolks and mix them with cut-up chickens and put them in, and, if you wish, small birds, and season

6. The pastries should be small and round, creating the effect of 'little cabbages', which is what the name means (< Fr *chou*). Other recipes call for other meats, such as veal or beef; some exceptionally rich versions include marrow. Fish-day versions substitute fish, and may call for almond milk.

your mixture well with sugar or honey. Then take cloves, maces, pepper, and saffron, and add them, and salt it, and then bake it and serve it forth.[7] (H279 VF, 35)

Crustade Lombard

Take good cream and parsley leaves and eggs, the yolks and the white, and break them into it, and strain through a strainer until it is so stiff it will stand up. Then take good marrow and dates cut in two or three pieces and prunes, and put the dates and and prunes and marrow on a pastry shell made of good pastry, and put the shell into the oven until it is somewhat hard; then take it out of the oven and take the liquid and put it in, and fill it up, and put enough sugar on it, and salt, then let it bake together until it is done. And if it is in Lent, leave out the eggs and marrow; and then serve it forth.[8] (H279 VF, 17)

Crustade of Herbs on Fish Day

Take good herbs and grind them small with a great portion of walnuts picked clean. Mix it with as much verjuice as water; boil it well with spice powder and saffron, without salt. Make a pastry crust in a pan and put in fish, unstewed, with a little oil and good spice powder. When it is half baked, add the sauce to it and bake it up. If you wish to make it without fish, boil eggs hard and take out the yolks, and grind them with good spice powder, and mix it with the sauce; and serve it forth. (FC, 164)

Noble Crustade

Take a baked pastry shell. Then grind pork or veal small with hard yolks of eggs; mix this with almond milk, and make it very thick. Take marrow from bones and put it in the shell, and fill it full of your filling, [and bake] and serve forth. (H279 VF, 36)

7. A 'Crustade', unlike a 'Flaun', is usually enriched with meat. Another widely circulated recipe for a simple 'Crustade' is based on veal, boiled in water and wine, and includes herbs as well as spices; one rather defective recipe for this type is labelled 'Crustade Open'. 'Crustades of Meat' are similar to this recipe, and a 'Crustade Royal' calls for marrow, dates, and currants in almond milk, thickened with egg. Some more elaborate variations are given below.
8. Fish-day recipes call for either fish or pears, and substitute almond milk for the eggs and cream (as do other Lenten versions).

Darioles

Take cream of cow milk, or of almonds; add eggs, sugar, saffron, and salt, and mix it all together. Put it in a pastry shell two inches deep; bake it well and serve it forth.[9] (FC, 191)

Dorrolette (Fish tarts)

Take minced fish and almond milk made with wine, and minced bread, sanders, honey, raisins, spice powders, and saffron; mix it all together so that it is thick. Put it in pastry cases and bake it as tarts. (OP, 128)

Douceties

Take cream and eggs, beaten together, with common raisins, and bake as you would darioles or flans.[10] (A1393, 21)

Flaumpoints

Take boiled fat pork; pick it clean and grind it small. Grind cheese and add it, with sugar and good spice powder. Make a pastry shell an inch deep and put this filling in it. Make a thin leaf of good pastry and carve small points out of it; fry them, and put them in[11] the filling, and bake it up.[12] (FC, 192)

Flaun (Sweet, plain custard tarts)

Take milk and yolks of eggs and draw this through a strainer with white or dark sugar, and melt good butter and add it, with salt; and make good pastry shells and set them in the oven until they are hard. Then take a peel with a dish on the end and fill the dish with your filling, and pour it into the pastry shells, and let it bake a little while. Then take them out and

9. Some recipes call for cheese or curds; a few add marrow and/or fruits. A Lenten version calls for almond milk, dried fruits, and almonds.
10. A more variable tart than Darioles. All other recipes call for sugar or honey; variants include currants instead of raisins, or neither; two use milk or almond milk instead of cream; one calls for chopped pork and several for marrow; one described as 'White' uses only the whites of the eggs.
11. Around, in a decorative edging.
12. Variants make such additions as eggs and dried fruits and nuts; fish-day versions substitute fish and ground figs for pork.

put them on a nice dish and sprinkle with white sugar, and serve forth.[13] (H279 VF, 18)

Flaun of Almayne (German flaun)

First take currants or other fresh raisins, and good ripe pears, or else good apples, and pick out their cores and pare them, and grind them with the raisins in a clean mortar; then add to them a little sweet cow's cream and strain them through a clean strainer. Take ten eggs, or as many more as will suffice, and beat them well together, both the white and the yolk, and draw this through a strainer; and grate good bread and add a good quantity of this, and more sweet cream, and mix all this together, and take saffron, and ground ginger and cinnamon and add this, with a little salt, and a quantity of good sweet butter. Make a pastry shell or two, or as many as is needed, and bake them a little in an oven, and put this batter in them, and let them bake as you would bake flauns or crustades. And when they are baked enough, strew on them ground cinnamon and white sugar. And this is a good manner of crustade.[14] (Ar 334, 128)

Great Pies

First slay your capon the night before, then plump him in hot water, then take him out to dry. Mince your stuffing of fresh beef with wine or verjuice or salt, to flavour that stuffing, and take suet, chopped, from that same beef and colour it well with saffron in a dish by itself. Then lay your capon in a fine pastry case, with a mallard beside it and two woodcocks. Put in your stuffing; with a hen, set egg yolks in it, then take your suet which has been well coloured and mingle it on top. Then colour your capon with saffron, using a feather. Then he shall be adorned with chopped dates, maces, and cubebs, cloves and grains of paradise and currants; then close the lid and pinch it, and bake it forth.[15] (LCC, 120)

13. 'Flauns in Lent' call for almond milk instead of milk and eggs, and include blanched almonds and ginger, sometimes other spices.
14. This is indeed more like a crustade than like a flaun. eM's 'Flaun Royal' is similar, but probably a little confused, telling us to mix an initial mixture of wine, eggs, and sugar into the pastry. H5401's 'Food of Life' is also similar, but using marrow and almond cream instead of eggs and cream.
15. Other recipes for similar 'great pies' agree that chopped or ground meat and whole poultry, of various kinds, are the essential ingredients.

Gurnard, Baked

Make a pastry case of the same length as the gurnard, except for two or three inches in which you shall turn the gurnard's tail. Lay it with the belly upward, and put in currants with pepper and cloves and three spoonfuls of rumney[16] or other wine, and if you wish, put in his belly a fresh eel. (H5401, 48)

Gyngile Tarts

Make like the tarts for the season of Lent, and instead of fish use meat.[17] (CCC, 15)

Leach Fries (Cheese custard tarts)

Take tender cheese; cut it in slivers and put it in hot, scalding water. When it runs together, take away the water as cleanly as you can and add a great deal of hot clarified butter and clarified honey, and mix it together well with yolks of eggs. Have pastry cases with rims as thin as you can make them and put in your filling so that the bottom is covered; let them bake at an easy temperature, and serve forth.[18] (OP, 135)

Malaches

Take swine's blood, flour, and diced lard; salt and mix. Bake it in a pastry case with white grease.[19] (FC, 159)

Paris Pies

Chop good butts of pork and butts of veal together, and put this in a pot and add fresh broth and a quantity of wine and let it all boil together until it is done; then take it from the fire and let it cool a little. Then add yolks of eggs and ground ginger, sugar, and salt, and minced dates and currants.

16. A sweet Greek wine.
17. The main difficulty it presents is that the preceding, presumably Lenten, recipe is almost entirely missing.
18. 'Leach Fries on Fish Days' (FC, 165) omits butter and honey (oddly, neither were generally forbidden on fish days) and adds ginger and sugar; 'Lenten Leach Fries' (FC, 166) substitutes almond milk for butter and eggs and sweetens with dried fruit.
19. 'Malaches of Pork', below, is filled with chopped pork, eggs, and grated cheese, and 'White Malaches' with eggs, bread, and butter.

Make good pastry cases, and put the filling in them; cover it and let it bake, and serve forth. (H279 VF, 27)

Parmesan Tarts

Take pastry of white flour and make a good container; take almond flour and fresh salmon and turbot and haddock and gurnard and luces and eels, maces and cloves and cubebs and ginger, cinnamon and dates and saffron, and flour and rice flour, and put it all in the oven. Take raisins and take out the kernels and drop them in, with good almond milk, and arrange them on top of the tart with blanched almonds and fruit, and bake it well, etc. (W1, 148)

Payn Puff

Make Payn Puff the same way you made Petty Pervant [20] but make the pastry more tender, and make sure the pastry of the Payn Puff is as round as a tart case or a pie. (FC, 204)

Pears in Pastry *see* Quinces in Pastry

Petty Pervant (A small, rich pastry)

Take marrow pared whole and carve it raw; ground ginger, sugar, yolks of eggs, minced dates, currants, a little salt – and be sure to make your pastry with yolks of eggs and that no water comes into it; and form your case and make up your pastry. (FC, 203)

Pike Pies

Take pikes and cut the fish in small pieces, and take out all the bones and the scales, then chop it small. Add to it currants, cloves, cinnamon, galingale, sugar, saffron, and salt, and minced dates, and eels cut into small segments. Then make large pastry cases, and take the belly pieces of salmon and lay them in them. Put in the stuffing with the eels in it and cover your cases. Bake them enough and serve them forth. (P, 210)

20.   See the following recipe – but it is not very helpful.

Pork, Malaches of (Pork pie with cheese and pine nuts)

Chop pork into pieces and mix it with eggs and grated cheese. Add strong spice powder, saffron, and pine nuts, with salt. Make a crust in a container; bake it well in this, and serve it forth. (FC, 162)

Porpoise, Baked

Salt the porpoise; parboil it well. Strip the skin off. Add ground pepper, and cinnamon if necessary: distribute on the fish, then enclose it in sheets of pastry. Bake venison in the same way. (OP, 121)

Quinces in Pastry

Make nice round cases of good pastry; then take good raw quinces and pare them with a knife and take out the cores. Then take enough sugar and a little ground ginger and fill up the hole, and put two or three pears or quinces in a pastry case, and cover them and let them bake. Lacking sugar, take honey, but then put in ground pepper and ginger. (H279 VF, 21)

Raphioles (Meatballs baked in a caul and pastry)

Take pigs' livers and boil them well; take bread and grate it; and take yolks of eggs, and make the mixture of these supple, and add to it a little lard, cut like dice, grated cheese, white grease, mild spice powder, and ground ginger, and make it into balls as large as apples. Take the caul of the pig and put every ball by itself in it. Make a pastry crust in a dish and lay the balls in that, and bake it; and when they are done, put in a thickening of eggs with strong spice powder and saffron, and serve it forth. (FC, 158)

Rastons (A yeast-risen 'cake')

Take good flour and the white of eggs and a little yolk; then take warm yeast and put all this together, beating with your hand until it is thick enough, and add enough sugar to it, then let it rest a while. Put it in a good place in the oven and let it bake enough, then cut a sort of crown around the top with a knife, and keep the crust you have cut off. Then pick all the crumbs inside together, and pick them small with your knife, and save the sides and all the crust whole on the outside; then put clarified butter in, and mix the butter and the crumbs together, and cover it again with the

167

crust you had cut away. Then put it in the oven again for a little while, then take it out and serve it forth.[21] (H279 VF, 25)

Lamprey Sambocade

Make a pastry crust in a container, and take curds and wring out the whey, and draw them through a strainer, and put them in the crust. Add a third part of sugar and some of the white of eggs, and shake into it elderblossoms; bake it up with rosewater, and serve it forth. (FC, 179)

Spynes of Fish (Fish tart)

Take good fish and chop them in pieces, and the liver with everything, and make a pastry case and put it in that. Grind ginger and pepper and saffron and add them, and cover it and bake it etc. (W1, 146)

Sturgeon, Turbot or Porpoise, Baked

Take a sturgeon, turbot, or porpoise and cut it in good pieces to bake; then make nice cakes of good pastry. Take ground pepper, ginger, cinnamon, and salt, and mix these powders and the salt together, and lay a piece of the fish on a cake and the powders underneath and above the fish; then wet the sides of the pastry with cold water and close the sides together, and set them in the oven, and bake them enough. (H4016, 173)

Tardpolane (Custard tarts with fruit)

Combine flour and sugar and mix into pastry with almond milk; make cases of this pastry two fingers in height. Then take pears, dates, almonds, figs, and raisins, and put in liquid and spices and grind together; add egg yolk and a piece of good, soft cheese, not too old, and plenty of whole eggs. Put them to cook; brush the tops with egg yolks, then serve. (AN A, 11)

Tart for Lent

Take figs and raisins and wash them in wine, and grind them small with apples and pears cleanly picked over. Take them up and put them in a pot with wine and sugar. Take boiled salmon, or codling or haddock, and

---

21. 'Bastons' (OP, 107), probably a variant spelling, calls for filling the loaf with honey.

grind them small, and add white powder [*see* Chapter 1, page 22, above] and whole spices and salt, and boil it, and when it is boiled enough take it up and put it in a container and let it cool. Make a pastry case an inch deep and put the filling in it; put on top damson plums, with the stones removed, and dates quartered and picked clean. Cover the case and bake it well; serve it forth. (FC, 175)

Tart in Ember Day

Parboil onions and herbs and press out the water and chop them small. Take green [freshly made] cheese and grind it in a mortar, and mix it with eggs. Add butter, saffron, salt, and currants, and a little sugar with mild spice powder, and bake it in a pastry case and serve it forth. (FC, 173)

Tart of Fruit

Take figs and boil them well until they are soft, then grind them in a mortar, and a piece of cod with them. Take them up and add currants to them; then add almonds and shredded dates, and take ground pepper and mix it in. Put it in the pastry case, with saffron above, and open them around the middle, and turn over the opening on the lid and bake them a little, and serve forth. (H279 VF, 11)

Tart of Meat

Take boiled pork and grind it small. Take hard-boiled eggs, ground, and add them with ground cheese. Take good spice powders and whole spices, sugar, saffron, and salt, and add them. Make a pastry case as before and put this in it, and cover with stewed small birds and rabbits, chopped into small gobbets. Bake it as before, and serve it forth.[22] (FC, 176)

Tart on a Fish Day

Parboil onions and herbs and press out the water and chop them small. Take eggs and add saffron and salt and currants, and mix in sugar and mild spice powder, and put it in a pastry case and bake it, and serve it forth. (H5401, 45)

22. 'Tartee' (FC, 172) is similar: omitting rabbits, it adds currants and plums.

Tart out of Lent

Take soft cheese; pare it and grind it in a mortar, and break eggs and add them, and then put in butter and cream, and mix it all well together; do not put too much butter in if the cheese is fat. Make a pastry case of dough and close it above with dough, and colour it above with yolks of eggs. Bake it well and serve it forth. (P1047, 22)

Tartelettes

Make small pastry cases; make your filling of boiled figs and spices, whatever you wish, or, if you wish, fish or meat, and season it up in the same way [as other tarts] and fill your cases with it. You may fry them, bake them – whatever you wish.[23] (OP, 120)

Tartlettes of Fish

Make small pastry cases and make your filling of boiled figs ground with spice powders, and fill your cases with this. You may fry them or bake them, and colour the lid with saffron. Place raisins on top, and serve forth.[24] (CUL, 82)

Turbot, Baked *see* Sturgeon, Turbot or Porpoise, Baked

Trap Desire

Take good flour and draw it with bastard [wine], and draw this with white of eggs; add sugar, saffron, and salt, and mix it together. Make a stiff pastry dough, and make your cases thin, low, and broad. Then take figs, dates, and raisins and grind them dry with a moisture of clarre; draw them through a strainer and season them with enough powder marchand [a commercial mixture], and put it in the pastry cases. Then make small holes in your cases and take raw egg yolks, and draw them through a strainer with enough sugar, and fill every hole full; set them against the sun as hot as you can, on hot lead, so that they will be baked enough. And always take salt of the bay, for it is made without fire. (Sl 7, 23)

23.   Other recipes prescribe veal or pork.
24.   No fish is mentioned.

Trap Sauce ('Filled crust')

Take two little earthen pans and set them on the coals until they are hot. Make a dishful of thick batter of flour and water; take one of the pans and grease it a little and put the batter on it, and let it run all around the pan so that the pan is all covered. Take the pan and set it over the coals again, and put the other pan above it, until it has baked enough. When it is baked, so that it will rise from the edges of the pan, take kid's meat and young pork, and chop it, and take parsley, hyssop, and savory and chop it small enough, and throw it among the meat and put it in the pan and the pastry shell; put it on the coals and let it bake well.

When it is done, take eggs and break them; take the yolks and draw them through a strainer. Add to the yolks white sugar, ginger, cinnamon, and galingale, and stir it well together. Take all this and set the pan down, and put it over the pastry shell in the pan; stir it together. Cover it again with that other pan and lay coals above, and let it bake well until it is done. Take it out of the pan, and take it out whole, or as much as you wish, then serve it forth. (H279 VF, 30)

Venison, Baked *see* Porpoise

Voutes

Take pieces of marrow and dates cut in large pieces, sugar, powdered ginger, saffron and salt; and make a leaf as you did before [i.e., an omelette], and take it out of the pan and make another. And take the stuffing and arrange it almost as wide as the leaf, and dampen the edges of the leaf and close it and bake it, and cut it in pieces, each piece two inches [5 centimetres] square, and serve it.[25] (NBC, 71)

25.   See the recipe at OP, 106 (and the adaptation there on pp. 186–7) for this stuffed omelette. (Voutes means something like turnover, from the French *volter* or *vautrer*.)

CHAPTER TWELVE

Fritters and other Fried Specialities

Apple Fritters

Take flour and eggs and ground pepper and saffron, and make a batter of it; and pare apples, and cut them in broad, thin pieces, and mix them in, and fry them in the batter with fresh grease, and serve it forth.[1] (DS, 19)

Blanched Fritters

Take blanched almonds and grind them all to dust without any liquid. Add to them ground ginger, sugar, and salt; put this in a thin pastry leaf, and close it in firmly. Fry it in oil; clarify honey with wine and bake it with this. (FC, 153)

Brawn Fondue

Take sliced brawn and yolks of eggs and some of the white and flour, and strain [the batter], and add to it a good quantity of sugar and a little saffron and salt. Then heat a pan with fresh grease, and take the brawn and wet it well in the batter and put it in the pan, and when it is fried a little take it up and put your liquid on it.[2] (eM, 63)

Brinews

Take wine and put it in a pot, with clarified honey and sanders, pepper, saffron, cloves, maces, cubebs, and minced dates, pine nuts and currants, and a little vinegar, and boil it on the fire. And boil figs in wine and grind them, and draw them through a strainer, and add them, and let them all boil together. Then take good flour, saffron, sugar, and clean water, and

1. This is the most common fritter; the recipes are entitled simply 'Fritter', apples being assumed. Other recipes add yeast and/or ale to the batter; 'Fritters in Lent' use yeast and omit the eggs.
2. The writer has forgotten to say what this liquid is; the title means the brawn is to be 'drowned' in whatever it is.

make cakes of this, and let them be thin enough; cut them into lozenges and put them in good oil and fry them a little while. Then take them out of the pan and put into a container with the syrup, and thus serve them forth, the brinews and the syrup in a dish; and let the syrup be liquid, and not too thick.[3] (H279 PD, 49)

Fried Brown Bread

Take brown bread and cut it thin, and then take yolks of eggs, with some of the white, and white flour, and draw the eggs and the flour through a strainer; and take a good quantity of sugar and a little saffron and salt, and add it. And take a good pan with fresh grease, and when the grease is hot take [the bread] down and put it in the batter, and turn it well in this, then put it in the pan with the grease and let them fry a little while. Then take them up and sprinkle with sugar, and thus serve them hot.[4] (H4016, 79)

Fritters of Pasternakes, of Skirrets, and of Apples

Take skirrets, pasternakes, and apples and parboil them. Make a batter of flour and eggs, and add to it ale and yeast, saffron and salt. Wet them in the batter and fry them in oil or grease; put almond milk on them and serve them forth. (FC, 154)

Cresterole

Take best white flour, eggs, and saffron and make pastry, colouring half of the pastry and leaving the other half white; then roll it out on a table until it is as thin as parchment and as round as a cake. Make it in Lent as well as in other times of the year, using almond milk [instead of eggs]; fry the cakes in oil.[5] (AN A, 14)

---

3. One earlier version calls for fried 'pellets' of flour and egg whites on a dish of chopped, boiled pig's intestines mixed with bread and ale, but all other versions are almost identical to this one.
4. It is likely that this recipe was originally a miscopied recipe for fried brawn.
5. The recipe doesn't explain how to make the cakes parti-coloured, if that is what is intended; at least one later version omits directions to make the pastry in two colours.

Crispels

Make a leaf of good pastry as thin as paper; carve it out with a saucer and fry it in oil, or in grease. For the rest, take clarified honey and baste them with this; arrange them neatly and serve them forth. (FC, 171)

Crisps

Take flour and whites of eggs, sugar or honey, and beat together and make a batter. Take white grease and put it in a pot and pour in the batter, and stir it until you have many parts, then take them up and serve them with the fritters.[6] (DS, 26)

White Crisps

Take best white flour and egg white and make a batter, not too thick, and put in some wine; then take a bowl and make a hole in it, and then take butter, or oil or grease. Put your fingers in the batter and put the batter in the bowl, and pour it through the hole into the hot grease; make one pancake and then another, putting your finger into the opening of the bowl;[7] then sprinkle the pancakes with sugar and serve with the 'oranges'.[8] (AN A, 2)

Cuskenoles

Make pastry mixed with eggs, and then take pears and apples, figs and raisins, almonds and dates; beat them together and add powder of good spices, and in Lent make your pastry with almond milk. Roll your pastry on a board and then cut it into many parts, each part the length of a palm and a half and three fingers in breadth, and grease your pastry on one side and put your filling inside. Each cake is a portion; fold them together as the diagram shows, and then boil them in clean water, and afterwards roast them on a griddle, and then serve.[9] (DC, 45)

6. None of the so-titled recipes suggest the outcome will be individual pancakes ('crepes'), but the earlier AN recipe (below) does, and perhaps later English cooks misunderstood it.
7. To stop the flow of batter when enough has been poured for one pancake.
8. Meatballs with a golden coating; immediately preceding recipe in the source.
9. The diagram is not very helpful: presumably the pastry is to be folded together and the edges crimped together. This is not a fritter or similar fried pastry, but it's not baked either, and this seemed the most logical place to list it.

Douce Desire [10]

Take blanched almonds; grind them, draw them up with fresh broth and sweet wine. Add a quantity of white sugar; put it in a pot and salt it. Take pork, well boiled and tender, and grind it small, and mix it with egg yolks, spices, and salt, and make pellets of it the size of the yolk. Have a batter of egg yolks and sifted flour and turn the pellets in this. Take them and fry them, rolling them in a pan so that they are round. Put them hot in dishes; put the sauce over, and be sure it is not too thick. And on fish days, you can use pike, haddock, or codling in the same way. [11] (OP, 44)

Emeles

Take sugar, salt, almonds, and bread, and grind them together; add eggs. Then take grease or butter or oil in a dish and anoint them; and afterwards [12] take them quickly out and sprinkle with dry sugar; make your emeles thus in Lent as at other times. (DC, 46)

Enaus

Take a mutton butt, pared away cleanly from the bones, and the suet around the kidneys, and chop them finely together with mint and parsley and other herbs cut fine together. Mix this up with egg yolks. [13] (RD12, 267)

Fig Fritters

Make a batter of flour, ale, pepper, and saffron, with other spices; cast them [figs] into a frying pan with batter and oil, and bake, [14] and serve. (H5401, 37)

Fritters Endored

Take marrow bones and break them; take out the marrow. Then take egg yolks and currants and dates, if you have them; mix all these together and work it with your hands as you would work dough for a pastry, and when it is well worked lay it on a board and spread it out about an inch thick; cut it

10. Cf. 'Diverse Desire', in Chapter 4, page 55, above.
11. This appears to be an elaborated version of one of the variants in Diverse Desire, which is given in Chapter 4.
12. Presumably after frying them.
13. The incomplete recipe ends here; the mixture appears to be one meant to be fried.
14. Fry?

in pieces the width of two fingers and a span in length. Then make a batter of flour and egg yolks and saffron; put each one by itself in the batter. Fry them, and put sugar and ginger on them, and serve forth. (CUL, 129)

Fritters of Cypres

Take raisins; cut dates in quarters. Pound figs in breadth and cut them in quarters, or smaller if you wish. Blanch almonds; mix them together. Spit them on pricks no larger than a rush. Make a batter of thick almond milk and prepared flour, and turn the fritter in spice powder and somewhat of salt. Let it all stick together well; then turn them so that they are well covered with the batter. Fry them, and serve forth as a fritter; strew on white sugar. (RD12, 256)

Fritters, Pork and Herbs

Take boiled parsley and sage with ground pork and a little honey, and yolks in the batter, and fry it. (A1393, 20)

Herb Fritters

Take good herbs; grind them and mix them with flour and water and a little yeast, and salt, and fry them in oil. And eat them with clear honey. (FC, 156)

Lombard Fritters

You can grind tender cheese and make fritters in the same way [as Long Fritters, below], and if you wish, take boiled pork, boiled until tender, and grind it with the cheese; make this into pellets as large as an egg. (OP, 109(2))

Long Fritters

Make as Samacays,[15] but without cream: see that it is stiffer. Lay it on a clean board that is no broader then your hand. Take a bone from the rib of a beast; wet it in grease so that your batter will not stick to it, and strike off the batter into a pan so that it will fall in small gobbets, every fritter a handful long, and serve them forth hot; and strew on white sugar.[16] (OP, 109(1))

---

15. Recipe below.
16. Some recipes simply call for cutting up the 'batter' with a knife. One, CUL, 116, 'Long Fritter Rapee', adds currants and minced apples to the mixture.

Lozenge Fritters

Make a long, broad pastry of eggs and flour, or else of egg yolks, and fry them abroad like a pancake; then make your stuffing of marrow and dates minced small. Or else take figs and raisins and boil them in ale, and strain them through a strainer. Or else take wardon pears; pare them, cut them up, boil them in sweet wine and draw them through a strainer. Then blanch almonds, chop them small with other pears, and mix them with the boiled pears. When they are cold, lay any of these three stuffings on the broad pastry and spread it out; close it with another cooked pastry, and cut it into lozenges [rhombus shapes]. Dip them in a batter made of eggs, flour, and saffron. Fry them well and serve forth. (CUL, 118)

Milk Fritters

Take curds and press out the whey clean; add to this some white of eggs. Fry them as usual, put on some sugar, and serve forth. (FC, 155)

Parsnip Fritters

Take parsnips and skirrets[17] and apples and parboil them. Make a batter of flour and eggs; to this add ale and yeast, saffron and salt. Wet them in the batter and fry them in oil or grease; add almond milk and serve it forth.[18] (FC, 154)

Round French Fritters

Take dates and marrow, chopped small; make it into small balls. Then make a batter of eggs and grated white bread and hard-boiled eggs and saffron; wet the balls in the batter. Fry them and serve forth. (CUL, 119)

White Fritters

Break eggs and keep the yolks whole in a container, then beat the whites well with your hand. Take tender cheese made of fresh milk; put the cheese in a mortar. Add to the cheese as much flour as you have cheese; mix it in

17. Another root vegetable, *Sium sisarum* or water parsnip.
18. Presumably almond milk is a sauce here. Another vegetable fritter, A1393, 19, calls for any of parsley (root), radish, skirret, or fennel.

the grinding with [the] whites of eggs so that it is somewhat thick. Gather it into a container. Make a lath five inches long; take it by the side and gather up the batter into lengths the same as that of the lath, and fry them yellow. Then gather them up in a container; set between them sugar, and give it forth.[19] (CCC, 76)

Froyse (Fried meat cake)

Take veal and boil it well, and chop it small, and grind bread, pepper, and saffron and add them, and fry it; and press it well on a board and serve it forth.[20] (DS, 18)

Gosnade (A fried green cake)

Grind together dried figs and dates and boiled pork; add to this raw eggs, so that it is not too thin. Add ground ginger, cinnamon, and saffron and salt; put it in a container. Make green colouring of parsley and mallows; when it is ground in a mortar mix these herbs up in the grinding with eggs and fresh milk. If this green colouring is not thick enough, mix in a little flour. Heat a frying pan and wet the pan with a little grease, using a few feathers. Put in it some of this green colouring, and then make a cake of it a span broad, and then take them up. Take one of them and lay it on a board; take the filling [i.e., the pork-based mixture] and fill half the cake to the thickness of a knife. Then take the other side of the cake and wrap it over, and close the sides together. Cut it and make it four-square.

Then take shelled eggs and beat together; add flour and make a batter. Then take your filling with the cakes [i.e., filled cakes] and fry them. But before you fry them, dip the side in the egg batter and make a sort of border of this batter about them. When you take them out of the frying pan, arrange them in a container and lay between them ground ginger and sugar. Give forth by themselves or with eggs in coker [cocker].[21] (CCC, 74)

19. Presumably the yolks are to be saved for another use? This recipe combines aspects of 'Long Fritters' and 'Milk Fritters', adding cheese to the basic ingredients of the latter.

20. The recipe in H279 calls for beef or veal, with eggs; its Lenten version includes rice, figs, raisins, almond cream, and several kinds of fish. H5401's version calls for pork and eggs; its fish-day variant calls for trout, barbel, or mullet, with eggs and butter.

21. 'Eggs in Cocker', page 141, above. 'Lozenges of Meat' (H279 LV4) is exactly the same dish, only not dyed green.

Mincebek (Sourdough fritters)

Take a third part of sourdough and flour with it, and beat it together until it is as tough as any lime. Salt it and put it in a dish hollow at the bottom, and push it out with your finger into a pan with oil and fry it well. When it is done, take it out and sprinkle with sugar, etc. (FC, 181)

Myles in Rapee (Fried balls of fruit and fish)

Take figs and wash them clean, and boil them in wine, and grind them small, and draw through a strainer; add ground ginger, cinnamon, maces, cubebs. Then take fresh salmon, or pike, or good fresh codling; boil it well and and pick out the bones. Then take cored pears and grind them very small with the fish; then take hard-boiled yolks of eggs and grind them with it, and put it into your container, and take sugar and ground ginger and mingle this with your stuffing well, and press it all together. Then make a good batter of almond milk and flour and add this, and fry them well in oil, and lay them on a dish and pour on the sauce, and serve forth. (H279 LV, 60)

Nuroles Farseys (Capon fritters)

Take a fat capon; mince and boil it. When the meat is done pour off the broth and add spices and yolks of eggs to mix well with it, and cook them in clear fat. (DC, 53)

Payn Perdu ('Lost bread')

Take bread of the day, or fresh bread; pare away the crusts. Cut it in slivers; fry them a little in clarified butter. Have yolks of eggs drawn through a strainer, and lay the bread in them, so that it is completely covered with batter. Then fry in the same butter, and serve it forth, and sprinkle on sugar. (OP, 110)

Rissoles (Pork rissoles)

Take pork; boil it and grind it finely with boiled eggs. Add good spice powders and whole spices and salt with sugar. Make small balls of this and put them in an egg batter, and put them damp in flour, and fry them in grease as fritters, and serve them forth.[22] (FC, 187)

22.   'Rissoles on Meat Days' (CCC, 8) is almost identical, adding herbs.

Rissoles in Lent (Fish rissoles)

Take figs and boil them in ale; take them when they are tender and grind them finely in a mortar. Then take almonds and shred them into this; take pears and shred them into this, too, and take well soaked cod or ling and tease that into it. Make your mixture, and roll it along in your hand, and lay them in flour; then make your batter with ale and flour, and fry them up brown in oil. In the same way make round fritters, which are called Ragons, and fry them up and then serve them forth.[23] (H279 LV, 48)

Rissoles of Fruit

Make pastry of flour kneaded with water; make a thin leaf. Have a stuffing of ground figs and raisins, and add clarified honey and a little cream of almonds, saffron and salt. Put it in the pastry leaf and enclose it; colour them with saffron, fry them in oil. Serve forth. (RD12, 260)

Rissoles of Marrow

Take good flour and raw egg yolks, and sugar, salt, and ground ginger, and saffron, and make nice cakes; and then take marrow, sugar, and ground ginger and lay it on the cake, and fold them together, and cut them in the manner of rissoles, and fry them in fresh grease and serve them forth. (H279 LV, 3)

Rissoles, Closed [24]

Take flour and eggs and knead them together; take figs, raisins, and dates and take out the stones, and blanched almonds, and good spice powder, and grind together. Make pastry cases a span in length and put your filling therein, a portion in every cake; fold them and boil them in water, and afterwards roast them on a griddle and give forth. (L553, 6)

Sage, Stuffed

Take pork and boil it well and grind it finely, and mix it with eggs and grated bread. Add strong spice powder and saffron, with pine nuts and

23. 'Rissoles on Fish Days' (CCC, 7) are similar but contain no fish.
24. Note that these 'rissoles' are not fried, but it seemed best to group them with the other rissoles.

salt. Take little balls of this and enclose them in sage leaves; wet them with a batter of eggs and fry them and serve forth. (FC, 168)

Samacays

Take curds before they are pressed; put them in a cloth and wring out the whey. Put them in a mortar and grind them well with sifted flour, and mix them with eggs and cream of cow milk, making a thin batter. Then have white grease in a pan; see that it is hot. Take up the batter with a saucer and let it run into the grease: draw your hand backwards so that it can run all around. Then fry them well and somewhat hard and brown, and serve it forth in dishes, and strew on white sugar. (OP, 108)

Sauterys in Lent (Fried ground salmon rolls)

Take raw salmon, ground; add ground pepper, ginger, and cloves, and saffron and salt. Make a leaf of pastry and cut it into slivers and fry them; add the fish, and mix them together. Make a thin batter of sifted flour and fresh water; make the fish into round rolls a hand long, turn them in the batter, and fry them up with oil. (RD12, 257)

Tartelettes in Fritter

Take figs and grind them small; add saffron and strong spice powder. Enclose them in leaves of dough and fry them in oil. Clarify honey and baste them therewith; eat them hot or cold. (FC, 157)

CHAPTER THIRTEEN

Subtleties and Drinks

A dinner in a substantial household would normally have ended with fruit and cheese, followed by spiced wine or other special drinks, often accompanied by wafers and, if the occasion warranted them, by small confections. The drinks which accompanied dinner would have been ale and ordinary wine: spiced wines were served after meals, like liqueurs after a formal dinner today, not with them. But also, an important dinner would have had at least one 'subtlety', usually the kind of confectionery art that survives in some of today's decorated cakes, at the end of the last course. The 'subtlety' might have been made of marzipan, and would have been fashioned to suit the occasion: like a modern wedding cake, decorated with a bride and groom; many of them featured a bird or animal, bearing a suitable motto. But some of them were simpler, like meatballs made to look like green (or golden) apples, and many other things were made out of the meatball mix.

Fruit would usually have been seasonal, although cooked fruits also appeared at this point in the meal, and some of them may have been preserved. Since no recipes are needed for fruit and cheese, these are not listed here: recipes for preserved fruits will be found under 'Preliminaries'. Many of the confections served at the end of the meal could have been purchased from professional cooks who specialized in such things, and only a limited number of such recipes will be given here. The first, 'Anise in Comfit', is long and repetitive; perhaps an experienced confectioner will understand it better than this editor does. It seemed important to include this recipe because it was the most popular of all the confections.

Subtleties

A Pastry Castle

Roll out a leaf of good pastry a foot broad and longer in extent. Make four pastry cases with the roller, each as big around as the smaller part of your arm and six inches deep; put the largest[1] in the middle. Fasten your pastry leaf with its mouth upward, and fasten the other four [to it] at each corner. Carefully carve out crenellations above in the manner of battlements, and dry the pastry hard in an oven or in the sun.

In the middle case put a stuffing made of pork with good spices and raw eggs with salt, and colour it with saffron; fill another with almond cream, and keep it white. In another, cow's cream with eggs; colour it red with sanders. In another, stuffing of figs, raisins, apples, and pears; keep it brown. In the other, the filling used for white fritters[2] and colour it with green. Put this in the oven and bake it well, and serve it forth with aquavite.[3] (FC, 197)

Cockatrice[4]

Take a capon and scald it and draw it clean, and cut it in two across at the waist; take a pig and scald it and draw it in the same way, and also cut it at the waist. Take a needle and thread and sew the forepart of the capon to the afterpart of the pig, and and the forepart of the pig to the hindpart of the capon, and then stuff them as you stuff a pig. Put them on a spit and roast them, and when it is done gild it with yolks of egg and ground ginger and saffron, then with the juice of parsley on the outside; and then serve it forth for a royal food.[5] (H279 LV28)

---

1. I.e., a square one made of that first large leaf of pastry. For a diagram of how to put the castle together, see the recipe in *Pleyn Delit*, no. 140.
2. See recipe under 'Fritters', page 178, above.
3. I.e., flambéed.
4. A fabulous beast, counterfeited by sewing the top of a cock to the hind quarters of a pig (i.e. 'gris': 'cockagris' is another word for this beast).
5. The version of this recipe in CCC is more elaborate, with different parts of the 'beast' variously coloured.

Eggs in Lent (Counterfeit eggs)

Take eggs and blow out the contents at the other end, then wash the shells clean in warm water. Then take good milk of almonds and set it on the fire; take a clean canvas and pour the milk on it, and let the water run out, then take it out on the cloth, and gather it together with a platter. Add enough sugar to it. Colour half of it with a little saffron and add cinnamon to this. Then put some of the white in the back end of the shell, and put a [yellow] yolk in the middle, and fill it up with the white, but not too full so it won't overflow. Then set it on the fire and roast it, and serve it forth.[6] (H279 LV, 39)

Pommedorry ('Golden Apples', i.e., meatballs)

See Farsure in Chapter 1, page 18, above (FC, 182)

Potwise (Flower pots made of meatball mix)

Take little earthen pots, of half a quart, and fill them full of the meatball mix for Pommedorrys [above], or make with your hand, or in a mould, pots of this meat mix. Put them in water and boil them well. And when they are done, break the pots and put the meat 'pots' on a spit and roast them well. When they are roasted, colour them as you would Pommedorrys. Make little bows of good pastry; fry them well in grease, and with them make ears to the pots, and colour them. Make roses of good pastry and fry them, and put the stalks in the hole where the spit was, and colour it white or red, and serve it forth. (FC, 185)

Sackwise ('Sacks' made of meatball mix)

Take small satchels of canvas and fill them full of the meatball mix for Pommedorrys [above], and boil them; when they are done, take off the canvas, roast them, and colour them, etc. (FC, 186)

6. The filling for these counterfeit eggs was also made with fish paste instead of almond milk. One version of this dish, using both almond milk and fish, Ar 334's jellied eggs, 'Eyren Gelide', calls for removing the shells after the 'eggs' are cooked and decorating them with gilded cloves.

Teste de Turk (1) (Turk's head)

Take pork and chickens and cut into small pieces, then grind in a mortar, and put in good spices and saffron; put in plenty of eggs, some bread, and some whole almonds. All these ingredients are to be ground together thoroughly in a mortar; then take a well-washed pig's stomach and stuff with the filling, and cook well. When it is done, take a skewer and pierce it through the middle, and remove the skin [i.e., the stomach]; then take egg yolks and beat them well with sugar in a bowl, and brush the roast all over, etc. (AN A, 26)

Teste de Turk (2)

A sheet of pastry [used as a case] well filled with rabbits and poultry, dates, peeled and sweetened in honey, new cheese, cloves, and cubebs; sugar on top, then a generous layer of ground pistachio nuts, the colour of the ground nuts red, yellow, and green. The head [of hair] should be black, arranged to resemble the hair of a woman, in a black bowl, with the face of a man set on top. (AN B, 27)

Teste de Turk for Fish Day or in Lent

Take choice rice and wash it and dry it, then grind it thoroughly and mix with thickened almond milk, and put in spices and saffron and sugar. Make a pastry case; then scald eels and remove the excrement, cut them up, and take parsley, sage, and some broth, and grind in a mortar, and put in saffron and mixed ground spice. Then cover with a [pastry] lid and put it in the oven, etc. (AN A, 23)

Urchins ('Hedgehogs')

Take the stomach of the great swine and five or six of pig's stomachs. Fill them full of the meatball mix for Pommedorrys [above], and sew them firmly. Parboil them; take them up and make small pricks of good pastry and fry them. Take these fried pricks and set them thickly in the stomachs on the filling, to resemble a hedgehog without legs. Put them on a spit and roast them, and colour them with saffron, and serve them forth. (FC, 184)

Drinks

Clarre and Braggot

Take ...7 cinnamon and galingale, grain of paradise, and a little pepper, and grind them, and mix this with good white wine and a third part of honey, and strain it though a cloth. [*To make Braggot*,] treat ale in the same way, but take eight gallons of good stale ale to one gallon of clarified honey, and heat three gallons of ale with the honey. Before it begins to boil, put in the spices; take it off the fire, stir it until soft, and let it cool. Then run it through a wide cloth sieve. Put it in a clean vessel with the rest of the ale, and put good brewer's yeast above, and hang the spices in the ale in a cloth, and cover it well;[8] and when it is fourteen nights old, drink it. (FC, 205)

Mead

Take honeycombs and put them into a very large container, and lay large sticks on them, and leave this weight on them until as much has run out as will do so; this is called live honey. And then take those combs themselves and boil them in clean water, and boil them well. Afterwards, press out of them as much as you can and put it into another container, into hot water, and boil it well and skim it well, and add to it a quart of live honey; then let it stand, well stopped up, for a few days, and this is a good drink. (GK, 9)

Pymente

Take one gallon red wine or white, for some love it red and some white. Add to it two pounds of honey and work it up in the same manner that clarre is made [see above]. Take the root of elena campana dry, two ounces, and galingale, long pepper, nutmegs, grains of paradise, cloves – of each, one quarter of an ounce. Rosemary, bay leaves, hyssop, mint, sage, six pennyworth dry; and make powder, and add it. (GK, 17)

---

7.   Quantity missing from manuscript; another recipe for clarre calls for 1 lb cinnamon, 12 ounces ginger, ¾ lb pepper, and smaller amounts of several other spices, along with 3 gallons of honey and a quarter pint of aquavite, for 20 gallons of clarre.
8.   Another recipe tells to also add aquavite to the braggot.

Ypocras (sometimes spelled 'Hippocras')

Take a half pound of select cinnamon; of select ginger, a half pound; of grains of Paris, three ounces; of long pepper, three ounces; of cloves, two ounces; of nutmegs, two and a half ounces; of caraway, two ounces; of spikenard, a half ounce; of galingale, two ounces; of sugar, two pounds. In default of sugar, take two quarts of honey.[9] (GK, 5)

9.   More complete directions would have told us to filter the mixture; the usual method was to put it in a bag and hang it up to drain into a clean container.

CHAPTER FOURTEEN

Wafers and Confections

Wafers

Take the stomach of a luce and boil it well and put it in a mortar with tender cheese; grind them together. Then take flour and white of eggs and beat them together, and take sugar and ground ginger and put all together, and see that your iron is hot; then lay this pastry on it and make your wafers, and serve them.[1] (H279, 24)

Anise in Comfit

Take two ounces of good anise and put it in a pan and dry them on the fire, continually stirring them with your hand, until they are dry. Then take them out of the pan and put them in another container, and take up your sugar in a ladle which holds an ounce, and set it on the fire, and stir your sugar with a wooden spatula; and when it begins to boil, take up a little of the sugar between your fingers and your thumb, and when it begins to stream at all it is cooked enough.

Then take it off the fire and stir it a little with your spatula, and then put your anise in the pan with the sugar, and continually stir the pan with the flat of your hand, slowly, on the bottom, until they come apart. But see that you stir them sharply so they will not cleave together, and then set the pan over the furnace again, continually stirring with your hand, and with the other hand continually turn the pan because of more heat on one side than on the other, until they are hot and dry. But see that it does not stick to the bottom. And when you see that it goes in the bottom again, take it off the furnace and continually stir with your hand, and put it on the furnace again until it is hot and dry.

---

1.   Wafers were, of course, made in wafer irons; a waffle iron is too big to use for this purpose, but many speciality shops can supply krumcake irons, which are of a suitable size.

In this way you shall work it up until they are as large as peas, and the larger they get the more sugar it takes, and put in your pan with each decoction.[2] And if you see that your anise becomes rough and ragged, give your sugar a lower decoction, for the high decoction of the sugar makes it rough and ragged. And if it is made of pot sugar, give it four decoctions more, and at each decoction an ounce of sugar: if it is more or less, it does not matter.

And when it is done at the latter end, dry it over the fire, stirring continually with your hand slowly at the bottom of the pan until they are cold, for then nothing will change their colour. And then put them in boxes, for if you put them hot in boxes they will change their colour. And in this way you shall make caraway, coriander, fennel, and all sorts of round confections, and ginger in comfit; but your ginger should be cut like dice in small pieces, four square, and give your ginger a higher decoction than you give other seeds. (GK, 12)

Chardequince

Take quinces and divide in four pieces with a knife, and take the flesh separated from the pips and boil it in a pan with clear water until it is very soft, then remove from the fire and strain through the middle of a strainer or sieve; and if there are 8 pounds of flesh, add 6 pounds of clarified honey, and put it over the fire and let it boil, stirring continuously until it is completely cooked, and test it in this way: take a knife, and take some of the mixture on the point of the knife and let it cool, if it is stiff, then it is cooked enough. Then remove from the fire and stir well until it begins to turn white; then add two pounds of eringo powder, 3 ounces of ginger, very finely chopped, and 6 ounces of ground ginger, and put all this combined into boxes and keep until needed.

And this way you can make Chardewardon [pear paste], Chardecrab [crab apple paste], and Chardedate, but the dates shall be ground in a mortar and not cooked, and the honey shall be cooked until it sticks hard between the fingers, and then put in the dates. And if you want to prepare it with sugar, put to one pound of pulp 2 pounds of clarified sugar, 2

---

2.   The word 'decoction' refers to the extent to which the substance is boiled down; how the cook is to manage this in this context is unclear.

ounces of spices, as stated above, except that you do not put in eringo powder. (G&C, 5)

Crab Apple Paste *see* **Chardequince**

Date Paste *see* **Chardequince**

Ginger, Preserved

Take one pound of the ginger called belendine and put it in cold sweet water for 12 days, changing the water every day; after 12 days, take one gallon of clean water and place in a pot, and add 4 ounces each of lily roots and green radish roots, cut very finely; 6 ounces of chalcanth and one pint of vinegar, and boil them all together until they come down to half a gallon. Then take them off the fire and let cool, and pour what is clear into an earthenware pot.

Take the ginger out of the water and put it in this pot, with the liquid, and let it soak there for 16 days; after 16 days let it be taken out of the pot, and put in fresh sweet water again for two days: the water should be changed twice a day. Then take it from that water and peel it, and when it is cleanly peeled, take one quart of skimmed honey and put in it 3 ounces of crushed ginger and the cleaned ginger, and let them stand together for 6 days.

Afterwards separate the syrup from the ginger and put it in a pot and boil it over the fire until a drop stands on your nail and does not fall; then take it off the fire and let it cool, and then let the ginger and the syrup be put together in one container and kept as long as you like, the longer the better.[3] (G&C, 3)

Gingerbread (confection)

Put half a quart of honey in a brass pan and boil it well over the fire, and stir it well with a wooden stick so that it won't stick, and let it simmer until it is as thick as wax. Then take a dishful of fresh water and drop some of the honey in it, and if it behaves like wax take it off the fire and dampen

3. 'Green Ginger' (apparently, fresh as against dried) was to be preserved in a syrup of white wine, egg white, sugar, and several spices.

a large wooden container well with water and pour in your honey. Take a pound of ground ginger and a quarter of an ounce of ground pepper and mix them well with the honey, and let it cool, and when it is cold take a pin of wood or of hart's horn and stick it into a hole bored in a tree with a gimlet, and take up the honey and draw it around the pin ten or twelve times, until it becomes as hard as tempered wax. Put it in a box and strew ground ginger over it, and this is properly made. (GK, 18)

Halakay

Take almonds and blanch them, then grind them in a mortar and make as good milk as you can. Boil it and add a little vinegar, then put it in a cloth so that it will be dry, and then put it in a good mortar. Add to it penides[4] and a portion of amydon, and sugar; and when it is ground, take out half to mix with gingerbread,[5] and this half portion shall be coloured with saffron and the other half shall be white. And when these things are cooked, put both in a dish, and on the white put pomegranate seeds or pitted raisins, and then give forth. (DS, 57)

Images in Sugar

If you wish to make images or anything of sugar that is cast in moulds, cook it in the same manner that sugar plate is,[6] and pour it into the moulds the way sugar plate is poured, but see that your mould is first anointed with a little oil of almonds. When they are out of the mould, you may gild them or colour them as you wish. If you want to gild them or make them silver, anoint them with egg white, and gild them or make them silver; if you want to make them red, take a little powder of brazil wood and boil it a little while with a little gum arabic, and then anoint it all around and make it red. And if you want to make it green, take two pennyweight of indebaudias,[7] two pennyweight of saffron, and the water of the white of two eggs, and grind it all together, and anoint it with this. And if you want to make it lightly green, put more saffron in it. And in this way you can

4.   A candy.
5.   No doubt the confection, above, not the cake-like version.
6.   Recipe below.
7.   Indigo.

cast all kinds of fruits, and colour them with these colours as diversely as you wish, and where the blossom of a pear or apple should be put in a clove, and where the stalk should be make it of cinnamon. (GK, 15)

Paste Royal (Sugar candy)

Take cleanly clarified sugar and put it in a clean pan, and boil it gently until it is of the consistency of quinces boiled to make quince paste. Then take it from the fire and put it in a topless container, and with a round staff stir it until it is as white as snow. Then add fine ground ginger to it and put it in moulds and set it in a suitable place to set. (OP, A.6)

Payn Ragoun (Sliced candied pine nuts)

Take honey and Cyprian sugar and clarify it together, and boil it over a low fire, and be sure to keep it from burning. And when it has boiled a while, take up a drop of it with your finger and put it in a little water, and see whether it hangs together. And take it from the fire, and add to it a third part of pine nuts and ground ginger, and stir it together until it begins to thicken, and put it on a wet table; slice it and serve it with fried food, on flesh days or fish days. (FC, 68)

Pear Paste *see* Chardeqeuince

Pears in Comfit

Take honey and boil it a little. Add to it sugar, ground galantine [8] and cloves, bruised anise, saffron, and sanders, and put in the pears, boiled and pared and cut into pieces, and wine and vinegar. Season it with ground cinnamon so that it will be brown enough. Make quinces in the same way, except the vinegar, and add cloves and maces; if you wish, take minced dates and add them, and colour it with saffron. (OP, 86)

Pokerounce

Take honey and put it in a pot until it becomes thick enough; skim it clean. Take ginger, cinnamon, and galingale, and add them; take white

---

8.　　Possibly meaning galingale?

bread and cut it into trenchers and toast them, and take your paste while it is hot and spread it on your trenchers with a spoon, and put pine nuts on them, and serve forth. (H279 LV, 36)

Pynade (Pine nut confection)

Wine and sugar, boiled together; gingerbread [the confection, not the cake] and honey, ground ginger and cloves; studded with great plenty of pine nuts, and shall be dressed in cases of chestnut flour. The colour, yellow with saffron.[9] (DC, 21)

Quinces in Comfit *see* Pears in Comfit

Sugar Plate

Take a pound of good clarified sugar and put it in a pan and set it on a furnace, and make it boil. Try your sugar between your fingers and your thumb, and if it does not stick to your finger and thumb it is now cooked, if it is pot sugar. And if it is finer sugar, it will have a little lower decoction. Then set it away from the fire on a stool and stir it constantly with a spatula until it turns from its brown colour into a yellow colour, and then set it on the fire again for as long as it takes to say an Ave Maria, while continually stirring with the spatula, and take it off again, but do not let it get over-stiff because of difficulty in pouring.

And see that you have ready beforehand a fine little marble stone and a little rice flour in a bag, shaking it over the marble stone until it is covered; and then pour your sugar on this as thin as it will run, for the thinner the plate is the fairer it is. If you wish, put in it any assorted flowers, such as rose petals, violet petals, clove pink petals, or any other flower petals: cut them small and put them in when the sugar first comes from the fire. And if you want to make fine sugar plate, put in it at the first boiling two ounces of rosewater, and if you want to make red plate put in it one ounce of fine turnesole, washed clean, at the first boiling. (GK, 13)

---

9.   The various recipes for this confection have little in common aside from pine nuts – and some of them substitute almonds for these. They vary from almond milk thickened with eggs (with pine nuts) to honey and ground radishes (with almonds).

Toast Royal

Take white bread and make trenchers of it, and toast them, and lay them on the side. For twenty servings,[10] take one quart of vernage[11] and half a quarter[11] of ground cinnamon drawn up with vernage, and boil it over the fire; add to it a quarter of sugar, a quarter of Paste Royal [a sugar candy], and one quarter of Chardequince, and mix it well. Add to it cloves, maces, pine nuts, currants, and minced ginger, and colour it with a little saffron. Take rice flour drawn up with wine and add it to the mixture to make it stable and thick, and in setting down that pot put in three ounces of ground ginger and a little rosewater. Then take the mixture and put it over the trenchers all hot, and take sugar plate and cut it into lozenge shapes and gild the ends, and plant the other end in the toast over the trenchers. Lay, for a lord, four trenchers in a dish, and serve it forth. (Ar 334, 204)

Tostee

Take wine and honey and mix it together and skim it clean, and boil it a long time. Add ground ginger, pepper, and salt. Toast bread and lay the sauce on it; carve pieces of ginger and decorate it with this, and serve it forth. (FC, 96)

10.　'20 messes', which would mean servings for 40 or more diners.
11.　A sweet Italian wine.
12.　Meaning a quarter of an ounce?

Bibliography

A1393   MS Bodleian Ashmole 1393; published in *A Gathering of Medieval English Recipes*, ed. Constance B. Hieatt, Brepols, 2008, Turnhout.

A1439   MS Bodleian Ashmole 1439; mid-fifteenth century; extracts published in *Two Fifteenth-Century Cookery Books*, ed. Thomas Austin (Early English Text Society, o.s. 91, London, 1888; repr. Oxford 1964), pp. 108–10.

AN A   MS B.L. Additional 321085; late thirteenth century; published in Constance B. Hieatt and Robin F. Jones, 'Two Anglo-Norman Culinary Collections', *Speculum* 61 (1986), pp. 859–82.

AN B   MS B.L. Royal 12.C.xii; early fourteenth century; published in Constance B. Hieatt and Robin F. Jones, 'Two Anglo-Norman Culinary Collections', *Speculum* 61 (1986), pp. 859–82.

Ar 334   MS B.L. Arundel 334; *ca.* 1425; published in *A Collection of Ordinanaces and Regulations for the Government of the Royal Household...Also Recipes in Ancient Cookery* (London, 1790); reproduction: Microfilm, New Haven CT, Research Publications, 1975; 1 reel, 35 mm. (History of Women, reel 80, no 519) xxii, 476 pp. Also in Richard Warner's *Antiquitates Culinariae* (London, 1791); facs. (London: Prospect Books, 1981), pp. 51–89. Both sources misidentify the MS as Arundel 344. (Warner's text was taken verbatim from the *Household Ordinances* edition.)

CCC   MS Corpus Christi College, Oxford F 291; published in *Cocatrice and Lampray Hay: Late Fifteenth-Century Recipes from Corpus Christi College Oxford*, ed. Constance B. Hieatt, Prospect Books, 2012, Totnes.

CUL   MS Cambridge University Library Ll.I.18; published in *A Gathering of Medieval English Recipes*, ed. Constance B. Hieatt, Brepols, 2008, Turnhout.

D55A   MS Bodleian Douce 55; mid-fifteenth century; extracts printed in

Two Fifteenth-Century Cookery Books, ed. Thomas Austin (Early English Text Society, o.s. 91, London, 1888; repr. Oxford 1964), pp. 115–17.

D55H   MS Bodleian Douce 55; mid-fifteenth century; extracts printed in Constance B. Hieatt, 'The Third Fifteenth-Century Cookery Book: A Newly Identified Group Within a Family,' *Medium Ævum* 73 (2204), pp. 23–42.

DC   MS B.L. Additional 46919; first quarter of the fourteenth century; published as *Diversa Cibaria* in *Curye on Inglysch, English Culinary Manuscripts of the Fourteenth Century,* ed. Constance B. Hieatt and Sharon Butler (Early English Text Society, SS.8, 1985), pp. 43–58.

DS   MS Bodleian Douce 257; dated to about 1381; once the property of Samuel Pegge, and published by him in the eighteenth century as an addendum to his edition of *The Form of Cury.* Published as *Diversa Servicia* in *Curye on Inglysch, English Culinary Manuscripts of the Fourteenth Century,* ed. Constance B. Hieatt and Sharon Butler (Early English Text Society, SS.8, 1985), pp. 59–79.

eM   MS Bodleian e. Mus 52; published in *A Gathering of Medieval English Recipes*, ed. Constance B. Hieatt, Brepols, 2008, Turnhout.

FC   *The Forme of Cury* survives in six MSS, with three close relatives; late fourteenth century. Published in *Curye on Inglysch, English Culinary Manuscripts of the Fourteenth Century,* ed. Constance B. Hieatt and Sharon Butler (Early English Text Society, SS.8, 1985), pp. 93–145. Additions and corrections in Constance B. Hieatt, 'Further notes on The *Forme of Cury* et al.,' *Bulletin of the John Rylands University Library of Manchester* 70 (1988), pp. 45–52.

G&C   MS Gonville and Caius College, Cambridge, 314/376; early fifteenth century; published in Debby Banham and Laura Mason, 'Confectionery Recipes from a Fifteenth-Century Manuscript,' *Petits Propos Culinaires* 69 (2002), pp. 45–69.

GK   A collection of miscellaneous recipes from various sources of the fourteenth and fifteenth centuries; published as 'Goud Kokery' in *Curye on Inglysch, English Culinary Manuscripts of the Fourteenth Century,* ed. Constance B. Hieatt and Sharon Butler (Early

English Text Society, SS.8, 1985), pp. 147–56. MSS with recipes printed in this group include: B.L. Royal 8.B.iv, *ca.* 1395; B.L. Sloane 121, *ca.* 1395; Bodleian Rawlinson D1222, *ca.* 1450; Corpus Christi College Oxford CCC F 291, *ca.* 1480; and B.L. Sloane 1108, *ca.* 1420.

H1605   MS B.L. Harleian 1605; published in *A Gathering of Medieval English Recipes*, ed. Constance B. Hieatt, Brepols, 2008, Turnhout.

H279   MS B.L. Harleian 279; dated about 1435; published in *Two Fifteenth-Century Cookery Books,* ed. Thomas Austin (Early English Text Society, o.s. 91, London, 1888; repr. Oxford 1964) pp. 1–56.

H279 LV   MS B.L. Harleian 279; dated about 1435; published in *Two Fifteenth-Century Cookery Books,* ed. Thomas Austin (Early English Text Society, o.s. 91, London, 1888; repr. Oxford 1964), 'Leche Vyaundez'.

H279 PD   MS B.L. Harleian 279; dated about 1435; published in *Two Fifteenth-Century Cookery Books,* ed. Thomas Austin (Early English Text Society, o.s. 91, London, 1888; repr. Oxford 1964), 'Potage Dyvers'.

H279 VF   MS B.L. Harleian 279; dated about 1435; published in *Two Fifteenth-Century Cookery Books,* ed. Thomas Austin (Early English Text Society, o.s. 91, London, 1888; repr. Oxford 1964), 'Vyaunde Furnez'.

H4016   MS B.L. Harleian 4016; dated about 1450; published in *Two Fifteenth-Century Cookery Books,* ed. Thomas Austin (Early English Text Society, o.s. 91, London, 1888; repr. Oxford 1964), pp. 65–107.

H5401   MS B.L. Harleian 5401; *ca.* 1490; published in Constance B. Hieatt, 'The Middle English Culinary Recipes in MS Harley 5401,' *Medium Ævum* 65 (1996): 54–71.

HU1   MS Huntington Library HU 1051; published in *A Gathering of Medieval English Recipes*, ed. Constance B. Hieatt, Brepols, 2008, Turnhout.

L553   MS Bodleian Laud 553; mid-fifteenth century, extracts published in *Two Fifteenth-Century Cookery Books,* ed. Thomas Austin (Early

English Text Society, o.s. 91, London, 1888; repr. Oxford 1964), pp. 112–14.

LCC — MS B.L. Sloane 1986. A collection of recipes in Middle English verse dating from about 1440. Published in Richard Morris, *Liber Cure Cocorum* (Berlin: Asher, 1862). Available online at http://www.pbm.com/~lindahl/lcc/parallel.html.

NBC — *A Noble Boke of Festes Ryalle and Cokery*, published by Richard Pynson in 1500, was the first cookery book published in English. It survives only in a unique copy in Lord Bath's library at Longleat. Two earlier manuscripts of the same collection are known, one of which was used by Mrs Napier in her edition published in 1882, transcribed (with many misreadings) from a manuscript missing a substantial number of recipes. Until a facsimile appears, readers are advised to see the list of contents in Constance B. Hieatt, 'Richard Pynson's *Noble Boke of Festes Ryalle and Cokery*', *Journal of the Early Book Society* 1 (1997), pp. 78–91, and to consult Napier's edition, with caution, for the recipes included there.

OP — MS Yale Beinecke 163, with several nearly complete copies in the B.L. and the Bodleian. Dating from about 1460; published in Constance B. Hieatt, *An Ordinance of Pottage* (London: Prospect Books, 1988).

P — MS National Library of Wales Peniarth 394 D; published in *A Gathering of Medieval English Recipes*, ed. Constance B. Hieatt, Brepols, 2008, Turnhout.

P1047 — MS Magdalene College, Cambridge, Pepys 1047; late fifteenth century. Published in Gerald Hodgett, '*Stere hit Well*', London, 1972, and Adelaide: Mary Martin Books, n.d. There are other editions of this book which may not have the same page numbering, and the culinary recipes are interspersed with other material, which may make it difficult to count the relevant recipes.

RD12 — MS Bodleian Rawlinson D 1222; published in *A Gathering of Medieval English Recipes*, ed. Constance B. Hieatt, Brepols, 2008, Turnhout.

Royal — MS B.L. Royal 12 B xxv; published in *A Gathering of Medieval English Recipes*, ed. Constance B. Hieatt, Brepols, 2008, Turnhout.

SA   MS Society of Antiquaries 287; published in *A Gathering of Medieval English Recipes*, ed. Constance B. Hieatt, Brepols, 2008, Turnhout.

Sl 1108   MS B.L. Sloane 1108; published in *A Gathering of Medieval English Recipes*, ed. Constance B. Hieatt, Brepols, 2008, Turnhout.

Sl 4   MS B.L. Sloane 442; published in *A Gathering of Medieval English Recipes*, ed. Constance B. Hieatt, Brepols, 2008, Turnhout.

Sl 7   MS B.L. Sloane 7; published in *A Gathering of Medieval English Recipes*, ed. Constance B. Hieatt, Brepols, 2008, Turnhout.

TCC0   MS Trinity College, Cambridge o.1.13; published in *A Gathering of Medieval English Recipes*, ed. Constance B. Hieatt, Brepols, 2008, Turnhout.

UC   MS B.L. Sloane 468; late fourteenth-century; essentially the same as MS Sloane 374, which is a little later. Published as *Utilis Coquinaria* in *Curye on Inglysch, English Culinary Manuscripts of the Fourteenth Century*, ed. Constance B. Hieatt and Sharon Butler (Early English Text Society, SS.8, 1985), pp. 81–91.

W1   MS N.Y. Public Library Whitney 1; published in *A Gathering of Medieval English Recipes*, ed. Constance B. Hieatt, Brepols, 2008, Turnhout.

WW   Wellcome Western MS 5650; published in *A Gathering of Medieval English Recipes*, ed. Constance B. Hieatt, Brepols, 2008, Turnhout.

Index of Recipes

This index includes names of recipes and editorial glosses on the recipe titles, as well as names of recipes referred to in the footnotes. It does not cover either culinary methods or ingredients in the recipes themselves.

acorn pottage, 28

alayed sops, 86

ale, sops in, with (bone) marrow, 86

allumells, 139

Almayne, flaun of, 164; haggis of, 97, 142

almond butter, 15

almond cream, 15; pork in, 100

almond milk, 16; pottage, 23; pottages based on, 23ff.; sops in, 86; spiced, 27

almonds, caudle of, 24

amydon, 16; (pudding), 23

amyn of meat, 47

anesere, 47

anise in comfit, 189

apple, apples: fritters, 173, 174; royal, 41n; tart, 157

applemoys, 41

appraylere, 93

aquapatys, 34

aquavite, 16

armanack, 139

aturmyn, 41

bacon: dried beans with, 34; gammon of, 93; with dried peas, 37

baked dishes, 157ff.

baked eel, 126

baked gurnard, 165

baked lamprey or salmon, 158

baked porpoise, 167

baked sturgeon, turbot or porpoise, 168

ballock broth, 64

barbel, boiled, 121

bardolf, 47

barleeg, 79

bass, 121

bastons, 168n

bean, beans: drawn, 34; dried, 16; dried, with bacon, 34; fried, 35; pottage, 34

bean blossom pottage, 28

beef: birds in sauce, 94; in gruel, 85; or mutton birds, 93; pudding, 94; tongue, 94; tongue, garnished, 95; roast, garlic sauce for, 148; roast, onion sauce for (syrup), 154; salt, 95

berandyles, 48

best sauce for roast chicken, 147n

better brawn, 79

birds: small or large, roast, 109; small, stewed, 48

birds (olives): beef or mutton, 93; beef, in sauce, 94

bittern, roast, 114

black sauce: for duck, 147; for roast chicken, 147

blancdesire, 48; mailed, 79

blanche doucet, 48

blanched fritters, 173

blancmanger, 49; accompaniment to, 27; gros, 49n; mole, 49n; of fish, 49n

boiled barbel, 121

boiled bream or roach, 121

boiled chicken, white sauce for, 155

boiled codling, haddock or hake, 122

boiled conger, turbot or halibut, 124

boiled cream, 141

boiled gurnard, 126

boiled mackerel, 128

boiled minnows or loach, 129

boiled mullet, 129

boiled perch, 130

boiled plaice, 132

boiled ray, 133

boiled salmon, 133

boiled sole, 134

boiled sturgeon or turbot, 134

boiled trout, 137

boiled whelks, 137

Bordeaux pie, 161

bours, 49

braggot, 187

braised fish, 121

braised sole, 134

braised tench or bream, 136

brandy, 16

brasee: eel in, 65; pike in, 130; tench in, 135

brawn: better, 79; de vine, 49; fondue, 80, 173; in comfit, 80n; in pepper sauce, 49; in peverade, 50; royal in Lent, 80n; sweet, 50; sweet and sour, 80, 95

bread: brown, fried, 174; drowned (payn fondue), 31; lost (payn perdu), 180; malasade, 143; see also sops, wastels

bream: boiled, 121; braised, 136; pasty, 160; roast, in sauce, 122; stuffed, 131

breast of mutton in sauce, 99

brew, roast, 109

brewes (brewis), chicken with, 113

brewet: cinnamon, 73; cold, 74; diverse, 71; eel in, 74; eggs in, 74; German, 74; German, in Lent, 75; German, white, 75; lamprey in, 75; Lombard, 75; mose, 72; of chicken, 72; of hare, 72; of kid, 72; of rabbit, cold, 76; oysters in, 76; pike in, 76; salmene, 72; salt eel in, 77; Saracen, 73, 77; sec, 73; Spanish, 77; tench in, 77; Tuscan, 77; venison, 78; whelks in, 78; white, 78; white Saracen, 77; without herbs, 73

brewis: in Lent, 86; in summer, 87

brinews, 173

brittenet, chicken in, 110

broiled salmon, 133

broth: ballock, 64; clear, rabbit in, 62; mussels in, 66; mutton, 59; sturgeon in, 135; venison in, 64; with eggs and bread, 30

brown bread, fried, 174

brown green sauce, 149n

bruce, 50

bukkenade, veal in, 105

bullace: pottage of, 41; preserving, 17

buntings, roast, 114

burnt food, amendment of, 17

butter: almond, 15; clarified, 17

cabbages: porre of, 38; pottage of, 35

cakes, tansy, 144

cameline sauce, 147

caper viaund, 140

capon: boiled, 60; fritters (nuroles farseys), 180; mange moleyn, 82 carpusselles, 51

carvel of pork, 61

cassels, chicken in, 110

castle, pastry, 184

caudle, 30; chicken in, 110; ferry, 30, 51; in chicken broth, 51; of almonds, 24; of mussels, 67; of salmon, 69; out of Lent, 24n

caul, meatballs baked in caul and pastry, 167

cayce, 51

celse, 51n

chardecrab, 190

chardedate, 190

chardequince, 190

chardewardon, 190

charlet, 52; coloured, 24

charmerchand, 52

chauden: for Lent, 65; of the wood, 28; pottage, 52; sauce, 147

chebolace, 35

cheese: custard, mon ami, 83; tarts (leach fries), 165; to soften that is too hard, 17

cherries: pottage of, 41; preserving, 17; stuffed, 41

chewettes, 161

chicken: boiled, white sauce for, 155; brewet of, 72; broth, caudle in, 51; compot, 53; endored, 109; florished, 109n; green pudding, 81; in almond milk sauce, 64; in brittenet, 110; in cassels, 110; in caudle, 110; in civy, 52; in concys, 53; in cretyne, 110; in dropeye, 55n, 75n; in dubatte, 53; in glass, 111; in gravy, 54; in guancele, 53, 149n; in herbs, 111; in hochee, 112; in kyslanes, 110n; in mose, 112, 53n; in musy, 54; in salome, 112; in sauce, 112; neck pudding, 80; pie, 161; roast, 103, 109, 113; roast,

a sauce for, 88; roast, black sauce for, 147; sauce for, 148; stewed, 113; stewed with beef, 114n; stuffed, 114; with brewes (brewis), 113; with pistachios, 63

chickpeas, pottage of, 35

chysanne, 122

cinnamon brewet, 73

civy: duck in, 115; haddock in, 127; hare in, 97; of lamprey, 127n; of ling, 128; oysters in, 67; plaice in, 132; rabbit in, 62; sole in, 134; tench in, 135

clarified butter, 17

clarified honey, 19

clarified sugar, 21

clarre, 187

clonnenonne, 140

closed rissoles, 181

cockatrice, 184

cockles, 66

cockles of cod, 65

cod, cockles of, 65

codling: boiled, 122; pottage of, 69

codling's head, stuffed, 122

cold brewet, 74

cold pottage, 24; violet or red, 24

cold tarts, 159

collops, of venison, stewed, 106

coloured cream, 25

comfit, anise in, 189; eel in, 125; pears in, 193

compot, chicken, 53

comyne, 25

concys, chicken in, 53

condiments, 147ff.

confections and confectionery, 189ff.

conger: boiled, 124; in pyole, 123; in sauce, 123; in service, 123

cooking without fire, 17

corat, 54

cormarye, 96

cormorants, roast, 114
coue de rouncin, 96
counterfeit eggs (eggs in Lent), 185
crab, 124
crab apples (chardequince), 190
crane, roast, 114
cream: almond, 15; bastard, 140;
    boiled, 141; coloured, 25
cream cheese, caper viaund, 140
cressadys, 31
cressee, 90
cresterole, 174
cretyne, 54; chicken in, 110
crispels, 175
crisps, 175; white, 175
crustade, 161
crustade, 162n; Lombard, 162; noble,
    162; of herbs on fish day, 162; of
    meat, 162n; open, 162n; royal,
    162n
crystal jelly, 89n
cullis, 54
curdling, milk, 19
curlew: boiled, 60; roast, 114
currants: and raisins, preparation of,
    21; macaroon, 43
cuskenoles, 175
custard: alayed sops, 86; egg, 142; pie
    (crustade), 161; pork custard tarts,
    160; small tarts, 160; tarts (flaun),
    163; tarts (flaun of Almayne), 164;
    tarts with fruit (tardpolane), 168;
    see also crustade
custard, cheese, mon ami, 83; cheese,
    tarts (leach fries), 165;
Cypres, fritters of, 177; viande of, 107
Cyprus: fritters of Cypres, 177; viande
    of Cypres, 107

dage, 55
dairy dishes, 139ff.
darioles, 163

dates: (chardequince), 190;
    (macaroon), 43; (white mawment),
    82
diacre, 55
diverse desire, 55
dogfish, stewed, 65
dorrolette, 163
dory in service, 124
doth, 141
double mortrews, 26
douce desire, 176
douce jame, 57
douce Saracen, 57
doucet brawn, 50
douceties, 163
doves stuffed, 115
drepe, 75n
dried beans, 16; pottage, 34; with
    bacon, 34
dried fruit tarts, 159
drinks, 187–188
drore, 75n
dubatte, chicken in, 53
duck: in civy, 115; in sauce, 115; pickle
    for, 151; roast, 103, 115; roast, black
    sauce for, 147; roast, sauce for, 152
dupercely, 96

eel: baked, 126; in brasee, 65; in
    brewet, 74, 125n; in comfit, 125;
    in gauncele, 74n; in gravy, 65;
    in sorre, 125; (leach proven), 82;
    reversed, 125; reversed, sauce for,
    148; reversed, stuffed with herbs,
    126; salt, in brewet, 77
eggs: egg dishes, 139ff.; in brewet,
    74; in cocker, 141; in Lent, 185;
    pench of, 141; poached, 141;
    pottages based on, 30; scrambled
    (hanoney), 142; with sage, 144
egredouce, 25; pig's feet in, 61; pork
    in, 100; rabbit in, 62; ramioles in,

104; tench in, 135
egret, roast, 115
elat, 142
elderflower pottage, 29
elena campana, with egg custard, 142
emeles, 176
enaus, 176
entrail, an, 97n
ermine, 25
eyren gelide, 185n

farsure for golden meatballs and other
   things, 18
fauntemper, 26
fawne, 28
feathered game dishes, 109ff.
fennel, sops in, 35
ferysse, 81
fieldfares, roast, 109
figs: fritters, 176; pottage, 42, 45, 46;
   tart, 157
fillets of pork: endored, 101; in
   galantine, 102
finches, roast, 114
fish and fruit, fried balls of (myles in
   rapee), 180
fish: braised, 121; fish dishes, 121ff.;
   fissoles (rissoles in Lent), 181;
   gaudy green sauce for, 149; jelly,
   89; spynes of, 168; tartlettes of,
   170; tarts, 158; tarts (dorrolette),
   163
flaumpoints, 163
flaun, 163; in Lent, 164n; of Almayne,
   164; royal, 164n
flounder (superpusoun), 135
flour, rice, 18
flour, wheat, to thicken sauce, 18
flowers, pottages based on, 28–29
food of life, 164n
founet, 96
four recipes for invalids, 85

freeshe of veal, 105
French: fritters, round, 178; joutes, 36;
   poach, 57
fried beans, 35
fried brown bread, 174
fried mullet, 129
fried pork, 102
fried sole, 134
fried specialities, 173ff.
fried spinach, 39
frissure, hare in, 97
fritter, tartelettes in, 182
fritters, 173ff.; apple, 173; blanched,
   173; capon (nuroles farseys), 180;
   endored, 176; fig, 176; herb, 177;
   in Lent, 173n; Lombard, 177;
   long, 177; lozenge, 178; milk, 178;
   of Cypres, 177; of pasternakes,
   of skirrets, and of apples, 174;
   parsnip, 178; pork and herb, 177;
   round French, 178; white, 178
fronchemoyle, fronchemolyle, 81n,
   97n
froyse, 179
fruit: and fish, fried balls of (myles
   in rapee), 180; custard tarts with
   (tardpolane), 168; pottage, 42;
   rissoles, 181; tart, 169
frumenty, 33

galantine: fillets of pork in, 102;
   lamprey, fresh or salt, in, 127; pike
   in, 130; porpoise in, 68; sauce, 148;
   sops in, 89
galingale, sops in, 89
game, 93ff., 109ff.
gammon of bacon, 93
garlic: chicken in yellow garlic sauce,
   53; pepper sauce, 150n; sauce,
   gauncele, 149; sauce for roast beef,
   148
garnade, 42

gaudy green sauce, 149

gauncele: chicken in, 53, 149n; sauce
  for goose, 149

German brewet, 74; in Lent, 75;
  white, 75

Germany: flaun of Almayne, 164;
  haggis of Almayne, 97, 142

giblets, a summer dish, 119

ginger: preserved, 191; sauce, 149

gingerbread (cake), 81

gingerbread (confection), 191

glass, chicken in, 111

godrich stew, 26

golden meatballs, stuffing for, 18

gole, pork in, 101

goose: gauncele sauce for, 149; in
  hochepot, 116; in porre, 116; in
  sauce madame, 116; petydawe, 118;
  roast, 113; salt (hare in worts), 98;
  salt, in porre, 116; stuffed, 114

gosnade, 179

grains, pottages based on, 33–34

gravy, 149; chicken in, 54; eel in, 65;
  enriched, 149n; oysters in, 67;
  rabbit in, 103; tench in, 136; white
  peas in, 37

great pies, 164

green peas royal, 37n

green sauce, 149

greynes, 148n

ground rice pottage, 33

gruel, beef in, 85

gruels and sops, 85ff.

gurnard: baked, 165; boiled or roasted,
  126

gyngile tarts, 165

haddock: boiled, 122; in civy, 127

haggis, 81, 97, 103n; of Almayne, 97,
  142

hake, boiled, 122

halakay, 192

halibut, boiled, 124

hanoney, 142

hare: brewet of, 72; in civy, 97; in
  frissure, 97; in papdele, 98; in
  sauce, 98n; in talbots, 98; in worts,
  98

haslets, 43n; on a fish day, 43

hawthorn blossom pottage, 29

hazelnuts: in season, 28; pottage, 28,
  59

head, stuffed codling's, 122

heppee, 28

herb, herbs: chicken in, 111; crustade
  of, on fish day, 162; eel reversed
  stuffed with, 126; fritters, 177;
  omelette, 142; pork and herb
  fritters, 177; preserved, 18

herbelette, 142; open, 143n

heron, 117

herring, stewed, 66

hippocras, 188

hochee, chicken in, 112

hochepot, goose in, 116

honey, clarified, 19

honey douce, 26

indigo (ynde), pottage of, 85

invalids, four recipes for, 85

jellied dishes, 89–90

jellied eggs, 185n

jelly: of meat or fish, 89; tench in, 90

John Dory, see dory,

joutes, 36; endored, 36n; French, 36

junket, 143

jussel, 30; with sauce, 30n

kale, pottage of, 36

kid, brewet of, 72

lampray hay, 43n, 158n

lamprey: baked, 158; fresh or salt,

in galantine, 127; in brewet, 75; sambocade, 168; tarts, 159; to salt, 19

lark, roast, 114

lasagna, 90

Latimer sauce, pike in, 68

leach, 89; bastard, 81; casuay, 98; cold, 42; fries, 165; Lombard, 82; lorrey, 82n; proven, 82; royal, 82n

leeks: boiled with mushrooms, 36; on sops, 88; porre of, 39; see also porre

leg of pork, sauce for, 151, 152

legs of pork: endored, 102; in green sauce, 102

Lenten greens, 36n, 40n

leach fries, 165n; on fish days, 165n

lete lardes, 83, 143

ling, 122n; civy of, 128

loach, boiled, 129

lobster, 124

loin of veal, larded, 105

Lombard: brewet, 75; crustade, 162; fritters, 177; mustard, 150; stew, 99

long fritter rapee, 177n

long fritters, 177

long worts, 36n

lorey of bullace plums, 41n

lozenge(s), 90; fritters, 178; of meat, 179n; on a fish day, 91n

luce in soup, 128

lupins, pottage of, 36

macaroni, flat, 91

macaroon, 43

mackerel: boiled fresh, 128; in service, 128; stuffed, 129

macrons, 91

madame, sauce, goose in, 116

makke, 34n

malaches, 165; of pork, 167

malasade, 143

mallard: in civy (duck in civy), 115; roast, 114

mange moleyn, 82

marrow (bone): rissoles of, 181; sops in ale with, 86

maundemene, 57

mawmene, 58; bastard, 58n; furnez, 58n; royal, 58n

mawment, white, 82

mead, 187

meat: jelly, 89; small tarts of, 160; tart, 169; to fasten two pieces of, 19

meat and game cookery, 93ff.

meatballs: baked in caul and pastry, 167; golden, stuffing for, 18; (pommedorry), 185; (potwise), 185; (sackwise), 185

meatless pottages, 23ff.; 31

mesegew, 43n

message, 43n

milk: against curdling, 19; fritters, 178; larded, 143; lete lards, 83; papins, 143; posset, 144; see also almond milk

mincebek, 180

minced onions, 19

minced veal in red sauce, 105

minnows, boiled, 129

mon ami, 83

mortrews, 58; double, 26; eweas, 58n; in Lent, 58n; of fish, 58n; of lungs, 58n; of whelks, 58n, 70; white, of pork, 62

mose, chicken in, 112

mounchelate, 58

mulberry sauce (murree), 149

mullet, 121

mullet, boiled, roasted or fried, 129

murree, mulberry sauce, 149

mushrooms: flourished, 37; pottage of, 36, 37

mussels: caudle of, 67; in broth, 66;

in gravy, 66n; in sauce, 66n; in
the shell, 66; porre of, 67; pottage
of, 66
mustard, Lombard, 150
musy, chicken in, 54
mutton: breast of, in sauce, 99; broth,
59; or beef birds, 93; pudding, 99;
shoulder of, in sauce, 99; steaks,
stewed, 106; stew, 58; stewed, 99;
tripe of, 59
myles in rapee, 180

noble crustade, 162
noble roast, 100
noble salmon, 133n
noumbles, 59; in Lent, 59n; of
porpoise, 59n, 69; of venison, 106
nuroles farseys, 180
nuts, pottages based on, 28–29, 59

offal, 59; see also noumbles
oil sops, 87
olyotes, 60
omelette, 139, 143; ; herb, 142
onion, onions: minced, 19; on toast
'sops', 87; pottage of, 38; sauce,
chicken in, 52; sauce, for roast beef
(syrup), 154; sops mare, 89; see also
civy
open lozenges, 91n
ouzels, roast, 109
oyster, oysters: in brewet, 76; in civy,
67; in gravy, 67; in gravy, bastard,
67n; (mussels in broth), 66;
pottage, 67

papdele, hare in, 98
papins, 143
Paris pies, 165
Parmesan tarts, 166
parsley sauce, 150
parsnip fritters, 178

partridge: and peacocks, 118; boiled,
60; in Saracen sauce, 117; stewed,
60, 117
pasta, 90–91
paste royal, 193
pasternakes, fritters of, 174
pastry: castle, 184; meatballs baked
in caul and, 167; quinces in, 167;
short, 19
pasty, bream, 160
payn: fondue, 31; perdu, 180; puff,
166; ragoun, 193
peacock: and partridges, 118; in
hauteur, 117
peapods, preserved, 20
pear, pears: (chardequince), 190; in
comfit, 43, 193; in compost, 44;
in rampant perre, 44; in syrup,
44; paste leach, 83; pearmoys, 43;
preserved, 20; (quinces in pastry),
167; tarts, 157
peas: dried, with bacon, pottage of, 37;
green, pottage of, 37; of Almayne,
37; porre, 38; split, porre of, 38;
white in gravy, 37
pellets, in Saracen sauce, 60
pench of eggs, 141
peony pottage, 61
pepper sauce: brawn in, 49, 50; for
veal and venison, 150; sharp, 150
perch, boiled, 130
periwinkles (mussels), 66
petty pervant, 166
petydawe, 118
pheasant: boiled, 60; roast, 118; sauce
for, 148
pickle, 150; for duck, 151; for pork, 151;
pike in, 130
pie, pies: Bordeaux, 161; chicken, 161;
custard (crustade), 161; great, 164;
Paris, 165; pike, 166
pig: in bars, 100; stuffed, 100

pigeon: roast, 118; sauce for, 151; stewed, 61

pig's feet in egredouce, 61

pike: boiled, 68; in brasee, 130; in brewet, 76; in brewis, 76n; in galantine, 130; in Latimer sauce, 68; in pickle, 130; in sauce, 76n, 131; in worts, 131; on sops, 87; pies, 166; reversed, 131n; sauce for, 151; stuffed, 131

pine nuts, candied (payn ragoun), 193; confection (pynade), 194

pistachios, chicken with, 63

plaice: boiled, 132; (chysanne), 122; in civy, 132; in sauce, 132

plover, roast, 114

plums, preserving, 17; white, 44; see also bullace,

poached eggs, 141; in sauce, 144

pochee, 144

pokerounce, 193

pomegranate pudding, 42

pommedorry, 185; (farsure for golden meatballs and other things), 18

pork: and herb fritters, 177; carvel of, 61; custard tarts, 160; fillets of, endored, 101; fillets of, in galantine, 102; fried, 102; in almond cream, 100; in almond milk sauce, 63; in a sweet spiced sauce, 57; in comfit, 100n; in egredouce, 100; in gole, 101; in sage sauce, 101; jagged, 55; leg, sauce for, 151, 152; legs of, endored, 102; legs of, in green sauce, 102; legs of, in sauce, 62; malaches of, 167; pickle for, 151; rissoles, 180; white mortrews of, 62

porpoise: baked, 167, 168; fresh, 68; in galantine, 68; noumbles of, 69; stuffed, 132

porre, 38; chaplain, 38; goose in, 116; of cabbages, 38; of mussels, 67; of peas, 38n; of split peas, 38; of white peas, 38n; white, 39

posset, 144

pot herbs, pottage of, 36

pottage, 27: ; acorn, 28; almond milk, 23; based on eggs, 30; based on grains, vegetables or fruit, 33ff.; based on nuts and flowers, 28–29; bean, 34; bean blossom, 28; brewets, 71ff.; codling, 70; cold, 24; cold, violet or red, 24; elderflower, 29; fish-based, 64ff.; hawthorn blossom, 29; hazelnut, 28; meat-based, 47ff.; meatless, 31; nut, 59; of ynde (indigo), 85; on a fish day, 45, 144n; oyster, 67; peony, 61; primrose, 29; rice, 33; rose hip, 28; royal, 45; summer, 63; sweet-and-sour (egredouce), 25; turbot, 70; violet, 29; wheat, 33; whelk, 70

potwise, 185

poultry and feathered game dishes, 109ff.

pourviens de hay, 27

powder fort, pouder fort, 35n, 50n

powder, white, 22, 35n

preserved ginger, 191

preserving: cherries, bullace or plums, 17; herbs, 18; peapods, 20; pears, 20; venison, 22

primrose pottage, 29

pudding: almond milk and rice flour, 26; beef, 94; bread and dried fruit, 27; chicken neck, 80; double mortrews, 26; dried fruit, 28; green chicken, 81; in Lent or on fish days, 69; mutton, 99

puff, payn, 166

pumps, 102

pymente, 187

pynade, 194
quail, roast, 118
quinade, 45
quinces: in pastry, 167; (pears in comfit), 193; pottage of, 45

rabbit: cold brewet of, 76; in civy, 62; in clear broth, 62; in egredouce, 62; in gravy, 103; in hodgepodge, 62n; in sauce, 103; in turbatures, 104; roast, 103, 104; two out of one, 104
raisins: and currants, preparation of, 21; on fish days, 45; pottage of, 46
ramioles in egredouce, 104
rapee, 46; bastard, 46n; of fish, 46n; of meat, 46n; royal, 46n
raphioles, 167
rastons, 167
ravioles, 91
ray: boiled, 133; in sauce, 133
red sauce, minced veal in, 105
rice, 33n; ; cameline, 33n; flour, 18; Lombard, 33; pottage, 33
rice, ground, pottage, 33
rissoles, 180; closed, 181; in Lent, 181; of fruit, 181; of (bone) marrow, 181; on fish days, 181n; on meat days, 180n
roach, boiled, 121; (chysanne), 122
roast beef: garlic sauce for, 148; onion sauce for (syrup), 154
roast birds, small or large, 109
roast bream in sauce, 122
roast brew, 109
roast chicken, 103, 109; a sauce for, 88; roast chicken or goose, 113
roast conger, 123
roast crane, 114
roast dory, 124
roast duck, 103, 115; sauce for, 152
roast egret, 115

roast gurnard, 126
roast lamprey, 127n
roast mackerel, 128
roast mullet, 129
roast pheasant, 118
roast pig, 100
roast pigeons, 118
roast quail, 118
roast rabbit, 103, 104
roast snipe, 119
roast sole, 134
roast tench, 137
roast turbot, in sauce, 137
roast veal, 105
roast venison, 106; fat venison, 107n
roast woodcock, 119
rose hip pottage, 28
rosee, 29
round French fritters, 178
rous, sauce, 153
royal brawn, 80n
royal tarts, 159
russntayles, 27
rysmole, 33

sackwise, 185
sage: eggs with, 144; sauce, pork in, 101; stuffed, 181
salad, 152
salmon: baked, 158; broiled, 133; caudle of, 69; fresh, boiled, 133; rolls (sauterys in Lent), 182
salome, chicken in, 112
salt, 21
salt beef, 95
salt eel in brewet, 77
salt goose: (hare in worts), 98; in porre, 116
salt lamprey, 19; in galantine, 127
salt venison, 22
salty food, amendment of, 21
samacays, 182

sambocade of lamprey, 168
samfarayn, 153n
Saracen brewet, 77; white, 77
Saracen sauce, 152; partridge in, 117; pellets in, 60
sardeynes, sauce, 152
sauce: beef birds in, 94; black, for duck, 147; black, for roast chicken, 147; breast of mutton in, 99; cameline, 147; chauden, 147; chicken in, 112; conger in, 123; duck in, 115; flour to thicken, 18; for chicken or pheasant, 148; for eel reversed, 148; for pigeons, 151; for pike, 151; for pork leg, 151; for pork leg, 152; for roast chicken, 88; for roast duck, 152; for swan, 154; for veal and venison, 150n; galantine, 148; garlic (gauncele), 149; garlic, for roast beef, 148; ginger, 149; green, 149; green, legs of pork in, 102; Latimer, pike in, 68; madame, goose in, 116; mulberry (murree), 149; parsley, 150; pepper, for veal and venison, 150; pepper, sharp, 150; pike in, 131; plaice in, 132; poached eggs in, 144; rabbit in, 103; ray in, 133; red, minced veal in, 105; roast bream in, 122; roast turbot in, 137; rous, 153; sage, pork in, 101; Saracen, 60, 117, 152; sardeynes, 153; shoulder of mutton in, 99; sober, 154; sorrel, 154; sylico, 153; venison in, 64; white, for boiled chicken, 155; without fire, 154
sauces, 147ff.
sauterys in Lent, 182
sawgeat, 144
scallions, pottage of, 35
scrambled eggs (hanoney), 142
sharp pepper sauce, 150

short pastry, 19
shoulder of mutton in sauce, 99
shrimp, 133
simple sliced dish, 78
skirrets, fritters of, 174
sliced dishes, 78ff.
slit sops, 88
small custard tarts, 160
small meat tarts, 160
snipe, roast, 119
sober sauce, 154
sole: boiled, roast or fried, 134; braised, 134; in civy, 134
sops: alayed, 86; and gruels, 85ff.; chamberlain, 88; chette, 88; dorre, 88; in ale with (bone) marrow, 86; in almond milk, 86; in fennel, 35; in galantine, 89; in galingale, 89; mare, 89; of salomere, 83; oil, 87; pike on, 87; slit, 88
sorre, eel in, 125
sorrel sauce, 154
soup, summer, 63
Spain, viande d'Espayne, 107
Spanish brewet, 77
Spanish dish, 47n, 63
spinach, fried, 39
spinee, 29
split peas, porre of, 38
spring onions, pottage of, 35
spynes of fish, 168
starch, wheat, 16
stew: godrich, 26; Lombard, 99; mutton or veal, 58
stewed chicken, 113
stewed collops of venison, 106
stewed dogfish, 65
stewed herring, 66
stewed mutton, 99
stewed partridge or woodcock, 117
stewed venison or mutton steaks, 106
strawberries, pottage of, 46

stuffed bream, 131
stuffed chicken, 114
stuffed codling's head, 122
stuffed doves, 115
stuffed goose, 114
stuffed mackerel, 129
stuffed pig, 100
stuffed pike, 131
stuffed porpoise, 132
stuffed sage, 181
stuffed wastels, 85
stuffing: for golden meatballs, 18; for
    hares, 98n
sturgeon: baked, 168; boiled, 134; in
    broth, 135; veal as counterfeit, 105
sturmye, 63
suade, 29
subtleties, 184ff.
sugar: candy (paste royal), 193;
    clarified, 21; images in, 192; plate,
    194
summer dish (giblets), 119
summer pottage, 63
superpusoun, 135
swan, 119; sauce for, 154
sweet and sour: brawn, 80, 95;
    pottage, 25; see also egredouce
sylico: sauce, 153; tench in, 136
syrup, sauce, 154

talbots, hare in, 98
tanne, 27
tansy: cakes, 144; in Lent, 145n
tardpolane, 168
tars curteys, 64
tart, tarts: apple, 157; cheese custard
    (leach fries), 165; cold, 159; custard
    (flaun of Almayne), 164; custard
    (flaun), 163; custard, with fruit
    (tardpolane), 168; dried fruit, 159;
    fig, 157; fish, 158; fish (dorrolette),
    163; fish (spynes of fish), 168; for

Lent, 168; gyngile, 165; in Ember
    Day, 169; lamprey, 159; of fruit,
    169; of meat, 169; on a fish day,
    169; out of Lent, 170; Parmesan,
    166; pear, 157; pork custard, 160;
    royal, 159; small custard, 160; small
    meat, 160; veal, 157
tartee, 169n
tartelettes, 170; in fritter, 182
tartlettes of fish, 170
tavorsay, 123n
tayle, 28
teal, roast, 114
tench: boiled, 135n; braised, 136;
    (chysanne), 122; in brasee, 135;
    in brewet, 77; in civy, 135; in
    egredouce, 135; in gravy, 136; in
    jelly, 90; in sauce, 135n; in sylico,
    136; roast, 137
teste de Turk, 186; for fish day or Lent,
    186
thin caudle, 30n
thrushes, roast, 109
toast royal, 195
tongue, beef, 94; garnished, 95
tostee, 195
towers, 145
trap desire, 170
trap sauce, 171
tredure, 30
tripe, of mutton, 59
trout, boiled, 137
turbatures, rabbit in, 104
turbot: baked, 168; boiled, 124, 134;
    pottage of, 69; roast, in sauce, 137
Turk, teste de, 186; for fish day or
    Lent, 186
turnesole, pottage, 84
turnips in pottage, 39
Tuscan brewet, 77

urchins, 186

veal, 151n; as counterfeit sturgeon, 105;
    freeshe of, 105; in bukkenade, 105;
    loin, larded, 105; minced in red
    sauce, 105; pepper sauce for, 150;
    roast, 105; stew, 58; tarts, 158
vegetables, pottages based on, 34ff.
venison: brewet, 78; collops, stewed,
    106; in broth, 64; in frumenty,
    34n; in sauce, 64; noumbles
    of, 106; pepper sauce for, 150;
    (porpoise, baked), 167; preserved,
    22; roast, 106; salt, 22; spoiled, to
    restore, 22; steaks, stewed, 106;
    with frumenty, 34n
vertdesire, 107
viande burton, 84
viande d'Espayne, 107
viande leach, 84; cold, 85
viande of Cypres, 107; bastard, 107n
viande royal, 107n
vine leaves, brawn of, 49
vinegrate, 107
violet pottage, 29
voutes, 171

wafers, 189ff.
wastels, stuffed, 85
weasels, 107
wheat pottage, 33
whelks: in brewet, 78; boiled, 137;
    mortrews of, 70; pottage of, 70
white brewet, 78
white crisps, 175
white fritters, 178
white malaches, 165n
white mawment, 82
white mortrews, 58n
white plums, 44
white porre, 39
white powder, 22, 35n
white Saracen brewet, 77
white sauce for boiled chicken, 155
wild goose, 119
woodcock: roast, 119; stewed, 117
worts: buttered, 40; hare in, 98; long,
    40; pike in, 131; pottage of, 39;
    white, 40

ynde, pottage of, 85
ypocras, 188